The Best of Being Catholic

The Best of Being Catholic

KATHY COFFEY

Maryknoll, New York 10545

Founded in 1970, Orbis Books endeavors to publish works that enlighten the mind, nourish the spirit, and challenge the conscience. The publishing arm of the Maryknoll Fathers and Brothers, Orbis seeks to explore the global dimensions of the Christian faith and mission, to invite dialogue with diverse cultures and religious traditions, and to serve the cause of reconciliation and peace. The books published reflect the views of their authors and do not represent the official position of the Maryknoll Society. To learn more about Maryknoll and Orbis Books, please visit our website at www.maryknollsociety.org.

Published by Orbis Books, Maryknoll, New York 10545–0302.

Manufactured in the United States of America.

Manuscript editing and typesetting by Joan Weber Laflamme.

Library of Congress Cataloging-in-Publication Data

Coffey, Kathy.
The best of being Catholic / Kathy Coffey.
p. cm.
ISBN 978–1–57075–978–9 (pbk.)
1. Catholic Church—Doctrines. 2. Theology, Doctrinal—Popular works. 3. Catholic Church—Customs and practices. I. Title.
BX1754.C484 2012
282—dc23

2012013631

For Sawyer Joseph,
my first grandchild . . .
only the best.

Contents

Introduction

Who are the most likely people to be interested in this book?

Many Catholics today are eager to know the best. After an avalanche of negative news, they're aching for something positive. "Counter the bad press my church has been getting!" they plead. Precisely because some feel this is such a tense and dispiriting time in the church, we must lift up again and with vigor what is best. Celebrating the good, we focus less on the negative which drains energy.

Some are thinking of becoming Catholic, exploring the church through the Rite of Christian Initiation of Adults. Through this process thousands of people annually become fully initiated Catholics. Some of what draws them is contained here. The questions at the end of each chapter will lead all seekers into more ownership and deeper reflection.

Others will see this title and cringe. "Doesn't this author know the worst of being Catholic?" they'll ask. "Does she not read the newspaper, know the horrors? How can intelligent women stay when they are devalued and disregarded?"

And some teeter precariously on the fence. Maybe they're drawn to some things Catholic, repulsed by others. In this category might fall young adults who admire the work for social justice but abhor the official stands on same-sex marriage, married and female clergy, or birth control.

One of the best lines in the Catholic Rite of Baptism is, "The Christian community welcomes you with great joy." Not with an agenda, a criticism, a challenge, a diatribe, a questionnaire, a wish-that-you-were-different or an exclusion. Instead, with the "great joy" of the shepherd who hoists the lost sheep onto his shoulders. This is a God more focused on love than on sin.

So the first words to all readers, including various configurations of the categories above: "Y'all come. Everyone welcome in the big Catholic tent." On different days the author finds herself in all three camps—and more. Such is being human: we lean; we step forward and backward; we slide; we skitter; we skooch; we change our minds.

In her poem "Mule Heart," Jane Hirshfield develops the image of a donkey carrying two baskets. One contains "the lemons and passion," all the fragrant blessings. The other holds "all you have lost."

Without becoming dualistic, it's possible to think of the church in a similar way. In one basket are the wonderful things: work for justice and peace; the saints; the Eucharist; the faithful followers; the creativity of art, poetry, music, and literature; the times we're proud to be Catholic.

For instance, when I hear a flute playing the theme from "The Mission," I recall the whole film. During the song "Gabriel's Oboe" comes the wry comment, "If the Jesuits had had an orchestra, they could've subdued the whole continent." Daring explorers and creative missionaries established in South America a place of culture and beauty where native peoples made instruments, played them, and sang in skilled choirs.

The whole beautiful enterprise was destroyed because of Vatican and government machinations. Yet what lives on isn't the duplicity or the violent attacks but the heroism of both native peoples and priests—classic examples of the best about being Catholic.

In the other basket rests what sickens and unnerves us: the hierarchical quest for power and control; the rigid attitudes that seem oblivious to raw, aching, human need; the silencing of the most creative thinkers; the preference for institutional law and custom to compassion; insensitivity to women; irrelevance to the young; a fixation on sexual issues clouding other vital concerns.

Because of these and other issues, a study done in 2010 by Robert Putnam and David Campbell showed that roughly 60 percent of Americans who were raised in the United States as Catholics are no longer practicing. The trend of "Latinization" (large numbers of immigrants from Spanish-speaking countries) is compensating, but retention among "Anglo" Catholics is hardly higher than for any other religious tradition.[1]

Oddly, the space between the two baskets is fluid. What once captivated—say, a moving liturgy—can become overly familiar and meaningless. A stance that once seemed woefully out of touch reveals its wisdom over time. Returning to our donkey metaphor: to ascend a rocky path or squeeze down a narrow one, the donkey needs the balance of both baskets.

When Jesus was threatened by Herod, he seemed oblivious. The tyrant couldn't influence him. But as Alicia von Stamwitz points out, Jesus was deeply saddened by the disaster of Jerusalem, the center of his sacred tradition. "For the first and only time, Jesus compares himself to an animal—a vulnerable, hopelessly faithful mother hen."[2] While he confronted authority fearlessly and critiqued the corruption of Judaism, he nevertheless remained loyal to the end, dying as a Jew with a psalm on his lips. Following his

---

[1] *American Grace: How Religion Divides and Unites Us* (New York: Simon and Shuster, 2010), 140–41.

[2] In *Give Us This Day* [a periodical published by Liturgical Press] (November 2011), 275.

lead, many people who have been hurt by the Catholic Church remain touchingly faithful to it.

God has always had a preference for working with the least likely suspects—the quirkiest, least suited to ministry or message. (For proof, one need only skim the Bible or the lives of the saints.) But somewhere in all the confusion we're grounded. And in that solid place is the best. It's a place worth exploring.

The following poem imagines what it must have been like to have been one of Jesus' first followers who made the decision—always an option for us all—to leave him.

The Turning

Because of this many of his disciples turned back
and no longer went about with him.
—John 6: 66

I whacked weeds
and hoed rows
fiercely, afterwards.
Flung a fishing line
with "Ha! Take that!"

He can't hook me
with silly schemes:
I resign! I was right,
too—poor guy crucified.
No thanks: I'll stay safe.

Nothing better than routine!
Then I remember: He didn't
run after us, cajoling.
I wonder sometimes,
was he sad to see us go?

When a late angle of
light bends over the lake
I miss the surprises,
the jolt of joy for a
woman's new-found coin.

Once a girl stirred and her
mother started cooking.
I long for his voice telling
stories, ache for abundant
invitations to larger life.

Part I

The Beliefs We Cherish

Introduction

The Inevitable Disclaimer

A SPACIOUS GOD

I live in Colorado where the skies are big, the mountains rear huge, the ski slopes filled with champagne powder extend for miles, and the summer lupine meadows are vast. The Creator of all this magnificence is too large to get snagged on denominational boundaries. Surely the great God transcends narrow fences and petty distinctions. As Joan Chittister writes, "God is too great to be lost in the smallness of any single sliver of life"[1]

So a book about Catholicism isn't meant to be narrow or exclusive. Anywhere that people have worshiped, prayed, or acted for justice is holy ground. We respect that human instinct to step away from self and praise the Creator, no matter the form of its expression. In *A Path with Heart* Jack Kornfield describes a man with an M.D. and Ph.D. who had studied the major world religions. What had he learned? "It wasn't the religions that had struck him so strongly, but the light that shines through them." All the great religions were "like screens placed over the great mystery of life."[2] Being genuinely Catholic means we also stand in awe of other ways to act, believe and meditate, honoring differences and respecting other religions as we would other languages or cultural customs.

A religious tradition, however, is a helpful construct for humans, a way to clarify who we are and where we stand. Certain foods, prayers, and music stir us to our roots—whether those are in Judaism, Buddhism, or Catholicism. Knowing where we're planted may help us to bloom more beautifully. This sense of identity certainly doesn't imply disrespect for any other tradition. Indeed, knowing our own good ground helps us appreciate other religions.

AND A PERSUASIVE PUBLISHER

Truth in advertising suggests that I should admit I haven't always been the best cheerleader for Catholicism. At times, I've been downright criti-

---

1 *Welcome to the Wisdom of the World* (Grand Rapids, MI: Eerdmans, 2010), 121.

2 *A Path with Heart* (New York: Bantam, 1993), 324.

cal. I hope that's in the best sense. As the *Dogmatic Constitution on the Church* says, "Laypeople have a serious obligation to express their opinions and insights about the Church" (no. 38).[3] I'm not the type to uncritically swallow anything that comes from the pope or bishops. I think the faith is important enough to demand serious reflection more than blind obedience. Many Catholic tensions and turf wars drain energy rather than offer life-giving spirituality.

So why am I writing a book like this? Blame Mike Leach, one of the most upbeat, positive people I know. He contacted me in utter delight about the book he was writing: *Why Stay Catholic? Unexpected Answers to a Life-Changing Question*. After its publication it took wings and became hugely popular. Mike's work taps his long personal experience as "the dean of Catholic book publishing." He has edited and published the full spectrum of Catholic writers, treating them all as if a mere clerical error stood between each author and the Pulitzer Prize.

As publisher of Crossroad, then Orbis Books, Mike Leach had shepherded four of my previous books into publication. Now, he wanted *my* spin on remaining Catholic. At first I was skeptical. How could I write more than a chapter on this topic? Furthermore, why would I want to compete with his book, appearing about a year before mine?

With typical ebullience, Mike brushed aside objections. "There's always room for more of a good thing!" he insisted. Gradually, I got caught up in his enthusiasm. I began to think of more and more things I like "best" about Catholicism. And little by little, a book grew.

It's possible that someone with a smidgen of skepticism can approach such a topic better than the full-blown enthusiast. I can understand fully some reservations about my religion, and sympathize with many objections. But still the stubborn tenacity insists there must be something wonderful that keeps me—and lots more like me—coming back.

I'm constantly reading things Catholic, and going to Catholic events. When I'm traveling, I miss my parish church. I'm always eager to return there. I was deeply touched when our choir members at a Christmas party sang the haunting refrain, "You are Alpha and Omega," so reverently that suddenly the drinking, joking, and general holiday hilarity stopped. In a few pregnant moments we remembered what Christmas was all about.

THE READER'S ROLE

I enjoy many friends, and Catholics make up part of that delightful, cantankerous, humorous company. There must be a great deal that's

---

[3] Unless otherwise noted, the translations used herein are from Bill Huebsch, *The Constitutions: Vatican II in Plain English* (Allen, TX: Thomas More Publishing, 1996).

"best" about being Catholic. As with every other exploration, a principle of selection applies. To the same place or question we all bring our individual background, experiences and opinions. One person, for instance, will relish the windswept beaches of the Outer Banks in North Carolina. Another, traveling to the same area, will be intrigued with the museum that celebrates the Wright brothers' first flight there. I became interested in the exploration of the church that follows—and hope to draw the reader into it too. The questions after each chapter invite personal investment and provide prompts for groups reading this book together.

QUESTIONS AT THE BEGINNING AND END

- What do you like best about being Catholic? (I asked this question in multiple interviews. Responses in "A Catholic Chorus" are scattered throughout this book.) As you read, keep this question and your response in mind.
- Then, at the end, ask which of your favorite elements the author has omitted and about what you agree with her.

Chapter 1

Homeless at the Broadmoor

A Tale of Astonishing Abundance

Fear is the cheapest room in the house.
I'd like to see you in better living conditions.

—Hafiz

Sometimes it sounds too good to be true. *We* (yup, limited and flawed as we know deep down we are) are made in the very image of the divine. Furthermore, God continues to dwell and act in us. Jesus once said something hard to believe: "The one who believes in me will also do the works that I do, and, in fact, will do greater works than these" (Jn 14:12). *Greater* things than Jesus?? But who are we to contradict *him*?

Such audacity stems from a long tradition. Catholics believe that from the beginning of time God has been creating a likeness, a people who would be a moving, active, visible image of God's invisible heart. In Jesus the divine and human met in a perfect marriage. As St. Athanasius said, "For the Son of God became man so that we might become God" (quoted in the *Catechism of the Catholic Church,* 460.)

Thus, everything we do is suffused with the divine. No longer is the deity a distant, punitive figure. The life of the Christian is grafted directly onto Jesus' life. As Pope Leo the Great said in a sermon, "He conquered that we too might likewise conquer."[1]

Jesus said, "I do not call you servants . . . but I have called you friends" (Jn 15:15). The human being isn't a slave motivated by fear but rather a child secure in the lavish inheritance: a meaningful life now and eternal life after death. In the Old Testament, Zephaniah says God "will rejoice over you with gladness, he will renew you in his love; he will exult over you with loud singing as on a day of festival" (3:17–18). This doesn't sound like a cranky, punitive God.

---

[1] Sermon XXXIX: On Lent I, available online.

The goal of *every* religion is joy, often defined as being fully alive and eventually being perfectly united with God and all creation. Over and over Jesus speaks of his mission to bring joy, and our call to receive it, to be joy filled. (Let's hope that focus hasn't been contradicted by too many cantankerous Christians.)

Paul writes, "When we cry, 'Abba, Father!' it is that very Spirit bearing witness with our spirit that we are children of God, and if children, then heirs, heirs of God and joint heirs with Christ" (Rom 8:15–17). Made in God's image, we are God's daughters and sons. No wonder that our slightest gesture can be filled with grace and light.

SACRAMENTALITY

While these scriptures are common to all Christians, Catholics push it one step further into sacramentality. We believe that Jesus sanctified everything and that God's presence everywhere continues to do so. So this conversation, this glistening lake, this friend, this turkey sandwich, this ordinary routine is holy.

Like the Jewish people, Catholics bless people, places, and objects not to make them holy—God has already done that—but to recognize the holiness already there. Because Jesus blessed the waters of the Jordan or the bread and wine at his last supper, *all* water, *all* bread, and *all* wine are holy.

A resident of Taos, New Mexico, once explained that the Rio Pueblo flowing across tribal lands from Blue Lake was sacred. "Then it crosses this fence," she gestured, "and it's not." In the Catholic scheme of things, as in the Native American, the whole river is holy—no boundaries to grace.

Even the less lofty parts of our life—the tragedies, disappointments, pains, and frustrations—can be better understood in the light of Christ's own suffering and death. As Paul Philibert writes, "Christ's triumph over death through his resurrection is our reason for hope in our moments of diminishment."[2]

OUR PLACE IN A LONG LINEAGE

One of the best things about Catholicism is a tradition that encircles the globe and reaches throughout history. If we have any tendency toward navel gazing, the church corrects it with a swift nudge beyond our small circles. Our liturgy and tradition uplift us into a universal culture of action, stories, art, and reflections. We are a people on the move, never stagnant,

---

[2] *The Priesthood of the Faithful* (Collegeville, MN: Liturgical Press, 2005), 30.

but pressing into eternity. Humbly, we take our place in a long procession, stretching back to Jesus and forward into the lives of our great-grandchildren. Here are brief examples of some of the finest links in a long chain:

> "Praised be my Lord God in all your creatures, and especially in brother Sun, who brings the day and its light. How radiant is your splendor. How like your Lord you are." —Francis of Assisi
>
> "Sin doesn't have the last word. Grace does." —Julian of Norwich
>
> "What a marvelous thing, that even while we are in the dark, we should know the light. That in finite things we should know the infinite! That even while we exist in death, we should know life!"—Catherine of Siena
>
> "What good is it to me if Mary is full of grace if I am not also full of grace? What good is it to me for the Creator to birth the Son if I do not also give birth to him in my time and my culture?" —Meister Eckhart
>
> "I die the king's good servant, but God's first. And I pray that we may all meet merrily in paradise." —Thomas More
>
> "I convened the Second Vatican Council so the human sojourn on earth might be less sad." —Pope John XXIII
>
> "To show great love for God and our neighbor we need not do great things. It is how much love we put in the doing that makes our offering something beautiful for God."—Mother Teresa of Calcutta
>
> "It is of little concern where in the chain we are. The important thing is to be in the chain, united with Christ."—Christian de Chergé

LIVING IN A FIVE-STAR RESORT

Sometimes we see our blemishes so clearly, but we can't quite swallow the fact of our magnificence. Or we've read/heard it hundreds of times, and it still doesn't sink in. For those reasons, metaphor may be the best—or only—way to understand things Catholic, especially the fundamental beliefs we hold most dear.

Since the dwelling symbol runs throughout scripture, this metaphor is useful for grounding such heady faith. Within the Father's house are varied rooms or "many mansions." In his poem "A Child of the Snows," G. K. Chesterton called heaven "the inn at the end of the world." Some people have gorgeous suites with traditional furniture; other styles are Art Deco. But everyone is under the same roof. So let's think of human magnificence in terms of a stunning resort.

The Broadmoor symbolizes every five-star hotel you ever wanted to visit but could never afford. Beautifully situated at the foot of Pike's Peak in Colorado Springs, Colorado, it has every creature comfort imaginable. The indoor pool has a glass ceiling etched with wildflowers that makes doing the backstroke like sailing through the art museum. It is, of course, surrounded with cushy lounge chairs and a steady stream of bounteous beach towels in matching colors. The outdoor pool has an infinity edge that leads the eye to the front range of the Rocky Mountains. Hot tubs are deep and soothing. As are the downy beds—acres of soft whiteness, like sleeping on clouds. The restaurants: ambrosia. The decor: gorgeous. The sunrooms: filled with flowers. The service: exquisite.

In summer, hanging baskets surround the lake. In winter, guests have drinks around huge fireplaces, indoors and outside. Women who've visited the spa have their friends practically weeping with longing for the aromatherapy, massages, facials, surround showers, water iced with citrus, trays of healthy treats. It's a romantic site for marriage proposals, weddings, anniversaries. Simply being there instills happiness, gratitude, nobility, and grace. Through such beauty, guests walk like royalty.

Now imagine being homeless: the day-in, day-out dreariness, the smells, the uncertainty, the hunger pains, the indignity, the unrelenting grimness, the ugliness. Children wear five layers of t-shirts to school, keeping all their clothing on because they don't know where they'll sleep that night. Hope for the future is "iffy," hinging precariously on winning the lottery. Few experiences could be so demeaning to the human spirit—and a clear end is never in sight.

If it's not too much of an imaginative leap, picture someone who'd been sleeping on sidewalk heating grates moving into the Broadmoor—an indefinite stay, all expenses paid. Leap over details like clothing; pull out all the stops of fantasyland. Focus on the joys: jumping up and down on the beds, making a cozy pot of tea or hot chocolate in the room, then strolling out to the balcony for a better view of mountains or lake, fingering with disbelief the monogram on the toilet paper, ordering a sumptuous breakfast in bed.

This isn't meant to be praise of consumerism or an uncritical endorsement of luxury. Remember, when we work with metaphor there's always some ambiguity in the mix. But in a loose sense, the comparison provides an analogy to the inheritance promised the children of God.

Even Catholic toddlers learn they are God's children. They know themselves beloved and precious to the great Lord of all the universe. And *that*, when you weigh thirty-seven pounds and have droopy socks, is an empowering message. Our true destination and authentic home, Catholics learn early on, isn't only the messy, violent, unfair world where we spend a lot of time, but the "many mansions" of the Father's house. Surely these will make the splendors of the Broadmoor pale.

And it's accessible to *everyone*. Saints who had nothing in their bank account, no frequent flier miles, and no immediate resort reservations record a deep happiness. Being with God—for them—is the equivalent—for us—of moving into the Broadmoor for free. Who *wouldn't* join poet Anne Sexton in her yearning, "I plead with it to be true!"?

The Broadmoor resort metaphor doesn't work for everyone. That's the nifty thing about the vast variety of rooms in the Father's house. Some may prefer to think of this inheritance as the ultimate dance floor, scuba diving reef, ski run, theater, electronics extravaganza, or symphony. Whatever the metaphor, it helps us imagine our own magnificence.

One of the finest themes, permeating good Catholic theology and literature, is *abundance*. Jesus overturned the eating taboos of his time to invite everyone to a sumptuous banquet. He walked among people who were probably diseased, smelly, and sweaty and assured them that even in poverty, mourning, or persecution they were "blessed"—the kingdom of heaven was theirs.

At times that's hard to believe. But as evidence within this life, we are given a taste of what makes us happy. It might be tennis, sewing, reading, cycling, singing, computing, gardening, building relationships, swimming, counseling, relaxing, cooking, playing cards, sky diving, creating an art or a business, teaching, running; the list is infinite. Small glimpses, in those activities where we lose track of time, foretell our essence and ultimate goal.

One of Jesus' followers many centuries later, Christian de Chergé, anticipated his murder at the hands of Muslim extremists. In his final letter to his family he wrote that he and his murderer were both "happy thieves," stealing paradise. In one sense we are all freeloaders, even those who pay for their room at the Broadmoor. For those given much, deserving little, praise should be a constant theme. The Bishops' Committee on Divine Worship writes, "The people of God . . . form a society whose task it is to praise." What a job description!

And it's not all pie-in-the-sky. Our high hopes for the kingdom don't stand in the way of daily, gritty work on earth to achieve God's justice for the poorest. That vision-in-process isn't simply of material luxury but of every human being knowing they are deeply loved, precious, noble. Even when the Catholic hierarchy can be legitimately criticized for exclusivity, there is a longer and better tradition of establishing and maintaining schools, hospitals, soup kitchens, AIDS treatment centers, help for immigrants, battered women's shelters, health clinics for the indigent, day-care centers. Indeed, the caring concern stretches back to Christ, who hung out with the marginalized, and to medieval monastic communities, who welcomed all guests as Christ.

Like any human family, the church has its whackos, the mean-spirited as well as the generous. If there are sixty-five million Catholics, there are probably sixty-five million reasons why they remain, and surely for some, it's nothing but apathy. But a plausible case *can* be made for thoughtful people to draw strength from the treasure house of Catholic spirituality.

The flaws are many and inarguable—no one could defend the "official" behavior during the sex-abuse scandals, for instance. Yet for each embarrassing example like that, there is a counterexample such as the women religious who prayed with Muslims after 9/11 and encircled mosques to prevent violent attacks. For centuries the church has stood against horrid brutality, oppression of the vulnerable, stupid warmongering, and the erosion of human dignity. It is our honor and privilege to take our place in that fine tradition. Some of the finest humans who ever lived have found Catholicism helpful—maybe we could too.

QUESTIONS FOR REFLECTION OR DISCUSSION

- Which of the Catholic beliefs described here—or others you know—strikes you as most astonishing? empowering?
- Does the metaphor of the luxury resort work as a way to describe the inheritance of God's children? If so, why? If not, what metaphor might work better?

A Catholic Chorus

Any choral group has its altos and sopranos, its star soloists, and maybe a few voices that are slightly off key. More important than their operatic quality, they ground one another. Attempting to sing without the other voices, they might sputter into silence. The harmony is essential to creating beautiful sound. To sing well, each vocalist must listen to all the other singers. Attuning to one another makes the music beautiful.

It's no different when people are asked, "What's the best part of being Catholic?" Each unique voice blends into the chorus. While the author might not agree completely with all those she interviewed, she respects their harmony and savors their individuality. She was also fascinated by the eagerness with which people responded. Those interviewed weren't necessarily uncritical; they knew the flaws of the Catholic Church but didn't dwell on them. To personalize the interviews, each speaker has been given a pseudonym. Vive la difference! is a motto that could well suit this Catholic chorus. Excerpts from their comments appear at the end of the chapters.

Chapter 2

The Stories We Tell

Sometimes a story's or movie's end becomes clear in the first three minutes. That man and woman battling so enthusiastically will, within two hours, inevitably wind up in each other's arms. Even in real life we can sometimes predict outcomes: the rich will get richer, and the poor will descend through spirals circling downward.

Maybe it's the tedium of the easily predictable ending that notches up our relish for Catholic stories. Ever childlike, we like the contrast to predictable entertainment, the jolt of surprise. By telling parables, Jesus used a storytelling tradition with the punch of the unexpected ending. It's a shame when overfamiliarity with the gospels blurs their funny twists and overturned-apple-cart conclusions. For as we all know, the stories we tell have a profound influence in shaping who we are and who we will become.

A tribute to this dimension of the faith is found in Steve Martin's "Atheists Don't Have No Songs," available on YouTube. The theme is that religious people create beautiful music and art; atheists have no good news to sing.

EXAMPLES FROM THE GOSPELS

The greatest storyteller ever was Jesus, who must've had a sly grin as the rabbis realized he'd filled the ceremonial washing jars with wine or spun a well-known ending into a form no one could've predicted. While "thinking outside the box" has become a cliche, he was gifted with finding creative alternatives to the stale solutions everyone else proposed.

For instance, when the religious authorities wanted to stone the woman caught in adultery, they put him "between a rock and a hard place." As Raymond Brown points out in *The Gospel and Epistles of John*, to agree to her death would violate Roman law—Jews didn't have the power of capital punishment. But advocating mercy would violate Mosaic code.[1] Instead of

[1] *The Gospel and Epistles of John* (Collegeville, MN: Liturgical Press, 1988), 52.

either solution, Jesus offered a third way. He hesitated, refusing to answer their question, drawing on the ground until the violence eroded. Always he respected the individual more than any legal demands. Gradually, the accusers dropped their stones. When we see his creativity, we too try to do things differently, more unpredictably.

One more passage explodes our expectations. The tone of the Advent readings is predictable: Be alert. Stand on guard. You never know when the king might come. It's all rather intimidating, and it certainly conflicts with the ideal: restful enjoyment of God.

Luke 12:35–40 starts with the same tone of dread. Jesus tells the disciples to be like servants awaiting the master's return, vigilant, ready to respond to his knock. Sounds threatening until we notice the details: the master returns from a *wedding*, that ancient symbol of unity and harmony. We know from the Cana story that the mood of wedding guests hasn't changed much from then till now. They return flushed, perhaps a bit tipsy, ready to crash happily.

That's why the master's action is so startling. He fixes a meal for the servants. Imagine their consternation: trying to rise, uncomfortable being served, upset at the normal order gone askew. They might have expected the whip cracked or a rigid inspection of the household finances. But gradually, they relax, enjoy the hot food, the full plates, the refills on wine.

This improbable meal echoes other gospel dining that lead to the Last Supper and eventually to our Eucharist. It's an invitation to outrageous abundance, and the only requirement is hunger. So preparation is done with delight, not dread. Perhaps the master will bring astounding surprises, not punitive doom. No wonder we eagerly await his coming. Any image of God that we wouldn't be drawn to spend all eternity with simply isn't God.

EXAMPLES OF THE SAINTS

St. Mary MacKillop

So that's how Jesus the leader does it. No wonder that his followers have continued on that path. The following true stories demonstrate God's sense of humor, wildly and radically spilling over our narrow rigidities.

From the outset, you'd assume that any struggle between a nun and a powerful bishop, especially in the nineteenth century, would end with her humiliation. Gotcha. An Australian bishop excommunicated Mary MacKillop, apparently for the audacity of wanting sisters to direct their own lives. In 1867, she founded the order of Josephites, who taught children in the Australian outback, where no one else had ventured to start schools.

At the time there were no free services for the poor, and young women flocked to join her work. Furthermore, Mary blew the whistle on an Irish priest abusing a young boy.

To put it mildly, the bishop—whose name seems mercifully forgotten, but who excelled at interference—was not amused. He began a rumor that Mary was alcoholic and tried to slander her in many other ways. The museum in Sydney dedicated to her memory has an animated diorama in which the bishop screams at the sisters and then throws them out on the streets of Adelaide. They had neither livelihood nor shelter—except what generous country people provided. Five months later, the bishop revoked the ruling as he lay dying.

Guess who was proclaimed the first canonized saint of Australia with her picture projected onto Sydney's Harbor Bridge 139 years later? At the announcement of *Saint* Mary MacKillop's name in Latin, the rowdy Aussies attending the Vatican canonization broke into a cry made famous when Australia hosted the Olympics: "Aussie Aussie Aussie, Oi Oi Oi!"

St. Catherine McAuley

St. Catherine McAuley, who founded the Sisters of Mercy, originally wanted her sisters to be "walking nuns." They needed freedom to be available to the poor, not cloistered as was customary in the early nineteenth century. However, she was forced into the only mold known to her time. After her training at the Sisters of the Presentation convent ended, she was so eager to leave she didn't even stay for breakfast. Over a hundred years later, her dream for lay people has finally materialized in the Mercy Corps, who minister in areas devastated by tsunamis, earthquakes, war, and poverty. It took a century to see her wisdom, but in the "big picture," the vision finally became reality.

St. Turibius/Oscar Romero

To be fair to the gentlemen, stories are "equal opportunity surprisers." A brilliant teacher at the University of Salamanca, Spain, Turibius de Mogrovejo's success was oddly rewarded. The law professor protested his appointment as bishop of Lima, highly unusual for a lay person. But he was quickly ordained a priest and a bishop, and then dispatched to Peru in 1581.

However, the new bishop did not act as the Spanish who sent him expected. He turned the tables by traveling throughout the country on mule or on foot. He found terrible oppression of natives by Spaniards, especially in the gold mines, and he spoke out against it.

His diocese was huge—eighteen thousand square miles—and he traversed it three times, learning native dialects, uncovering abuse, and founding hospitals, schools, and churches. Probably astonishing himself as much as anyone else, Turibius served in his unexpected role for twenty-six years. He was determined that Peruvians see a better side of Christianity than that practiced by colonial powers. In him, they did.

A similar conversion happened for Archbishop Oscar Romero of El Salvador. He was elected on the assumption that he'd be safe and conservative, looking out for the interests of the church and the oligarchy. What a shock when, after the death of his friend Rutilio Grande, SJ, he sided with the poor, and his regular radio broadcasts called for an end to war and the violence of the military thugs.

Division among peoples, doubts about a prophet, and opposition to authorities weren't new trends in the sixteenth century: the same themes, especially skepticism about Jesus, pervade the gospel.

ASSORTED QUIRKS

Lisa Wangsness recounts a turn-the-tables story in the December 26, 2010, issue of the *Boston Globe.* When Cardinal Sean O'Malley was just out of seminary, he preached his first sermon to inmates at a county prison. O'Malley jazzed up the homily with lively escape stories from the Bible: Daniel, St. Paul, St. Peter. The audience was enraptured; that night, inspired, several escaped. Despite the outrage of his superior, O'Malley has continued prison ministry. He explains: "My presence there is a signal to them that they are not forgotten, that they are important to the church, that they are part of our family."

One of the quirkiest, ongoing Catholic stories is the discrepancy between official positions and lived realities. For example, while the Vatican fulminated that all bibles and sacred texts *must* be in Latin, Jesuits were quietly translating the Bible into the languages of Asia and Africa, bringing good news everywhere they ministered, in ways people could understand. Father Pierron, first Jesuit missionary to the Mohawk community where St. Kateri Tekakwitha became Catholic, didn't speak the language but painted scenes from Christ's life on linen.

A similar attempt occurred before Vatican II. Ordering that Latin would be *the* church language, hierarchs directed that all seminary classes be taught in it—even Algebra. Teachers and students were equally flummoxed, but it didn't last long. The council "opened the windows" so wide that even the mass moved into the vernacular language. The open window might be a fitting symbol for a church that hasn't always welcomed the fresh air of change. But when it does, it's at its best.

EXAMPLES FROM CONTEMPORARY FILMS

"Of Gods and Men"

When asked, "What's your favorite part of being Catholic?" one person replied immediately, "Of Gods and Men"! She referred to a film loosely based on the story of Trappists killed in Algeria in 1996. As a young man, Christian de Chergé, their prior, had done his compulsory military service working with civilians in Algeria. He was impressed that he could speak freely about God with Muslims, in contrast to his native France, where God-talk made people uncomfortable.

One friend—Mohammed, the father of ten, who shared a common love of God—intervened when thugs aimed their rifles at Christian. Because he defended Christian as a godly man. Mohammed was killed that night. Christian later wrote his community, "In the blood shed by this friend, who was assassinated because he would not practice hatred, I knew that my call to follow Christ would be lived sooner or later in the same country that gave me a tangible sign of the greatest love possible." Christian resumed his studies for the priesthood, adding intense study of the Qur'an.

He then moved to an ideal abbey in Algeria, which by 1867 had gained a reputation for model agriculture and production of fine wines. Good neighbors, the monks also fed starving Muslims during the famines of 1847 and 1867. Under Christian's leadership the monks continued to offer a safe space for respectful Muslim-Christian dialogue and prayer. He sought "the notes that are in harmony" between Christianity and Islam.

The film reveals a life following the monastic ideal: *laborare et orare* (work and pray). Even when helicopters circled menacingly over the monastery, the monks linked arms and sang a hymn together. This is Catholic liturgy at its finest—subtly uniting a disparate group and working its alchemy on their souls.

A realistic, human note is the monks' disagreement about whether to remain in the country as threats to foreigners escalated. Clearly an integral part of their village, they attended Muslim family events and farmed. Luc, the doctor in their group, provided much needed medical care, and villagers saw their presence as a protection. When one monk said, "We're like birds on a branch—we don't know if we'll be leaving," a Muslim woman complimented their commitment: "We're the birds. You're the branch."

Some were ambivalent about staying to face almost certain death. One voiced it bluntly: "I didn't come here to commit collective suicide." Their hesitation was respected and honestly discussed. As Father Paul asked, "How far does one go to save his skin without running the risk of losing his soul?" Eventually all came to peace with the decision to stay, realizing that they rested in God's embrace.

In a scene near the end of the film that echoes the Last Supper, they listen to the music of "Swan Lake." Good Frenchmen, they sipped red wine appreciatively. No words were necessary; their faces showed them loving the best of this world and at the same time preparing to leave it.

While monasticism may not be the preferred spirituality of most people in the twenty-first century, it inspires the rest of us to live with just as much conviction and dedication. We may not be martyrs in foreign countries, but we follow the same Lord. Christ calls us all to be transformed into himself, whatever the diverse paths by which we reach him.

"The Way"

The theme of pilgrimage has been a Catholic constant—remember *The Canterbury Tales*? In this classic of Middle English, Chaucer uses a pilgrimage to the shrine of St. Thomas Beckett in England as the vehicle to present captivating characters—like the Wife of Bath—who tell stories that are often raunchy.

Joyce Rupp's book *Walk in a Relaxed Manner: Life Lessons from the Camino* describes her experience on ancient path through northern Spain to the shrine of Santiago de Compostela, where some believe St. James is buried.[2] From the tenth century onward, pilgrims have walked this route, with up to a million people following it during the Middle Ages.

Today people of many nationalities and all or no religions continue the tradition. Lodging along the way is often dirty, primitive, and totally lacking in privacy. Finding food can be problematic; the weather can be rainy, cold, or blistering hot; the backpacks grow heavy; and blisters on the feet are legendary. Why then do over one thousand people a day in summer begin the pilgrimage?

Answers vary, but Rupp sums up some. Pilgrims want to be empowered by the energizing presence of so many who have walked the sacred way before them. They want to travel light, discovering they can survive for weeks with a carefully stocked backpack. They enjoy a simplicity unknown in their usual complex lifestyles. They even lose their titles and accomplishments; identified only by first names, they share their essential humanity. Meeting and befriending other pilgrims from many countries is a big plus. Even the language barrier can't prevent exuberant sharing of meals at the end of each day.

---

[2] Maryknoll, NY: Orbis Books, 2005.

The broader implications are that one better appreciates life as a road, just as sacred and full of opportunities for growth and gratitude. On pilgrimage, as in life, one is ideally transformed into one's best self.

Director Emilio Estevez's film "The Way" gives faces to these ideas. Martin Sheen plays Tom, a father whose estranged son, Daniel, died on the first day of his pilgrimage. When Tom comes to claim his only child's body, he decides to complete the pilgrimage with Daniel's ashes in his backpack. It becomes a ritual for Tom to scatter ashes at markers along the way. Tom had once criticized Daniel for not finishing his doctorate and contributing to the world. The son had suggested, in turn, that the father needed to travel more. Along the way, Tom imagines his son's presence, perhaps encouraging him to become broader in a most unlikely setting.

As Tom walks, he joins three companions whom he first resents, but who eventually become his friends. Each one carries a hidden agenda and a secret suffering; Tom's is the most visible. Each also carries a shell, the traditional symbol of the pilgrim; its origins have become lost in history. At the end they do not accomplish their stated goals. But they do learn to live (humorously) with their flaws.

At St. James Cathedral they stand before a pillar filled with carvings of the Jesse tree, the symbolic lineage of Jesus. They place their hands within prints worn by millions before them. They receive diplomas of completion, which Tom deliberately changes from his name into Daniel's. During mass they watch a censor *(botafumeiro)* so massive it takes several men with ropes to swing it high and wide. One explanation for this tradition is that it arose as an attempt to cover the stench of the pilgrims, who hadn't washed for some time. This exaggeration of the incensing sometimes done in Catholic ritual with smaller vessels could also symbolize that it's *all* sacred ground, all the ups and downs. The whole, long path of life is blessed.

The film demonstrates that the Camino isn't about arrival at a destination but about what happens along the way. As Rupp says, it's hard to stop walking when the rhythm has become part of the body. So the foursome continues a relatively short distance to the sea, where Tom scatters the last of Daniel's ashes. The church had become for the group's Irish writer a "temple of tears." It doesn't seem like the proper or final destination. But the sea represents the majestic sweep of the Creator; there, Tom can finally lay his son to rest.

QUESTIONS FOR REFLECTION OR DISCUSSION

- What are your favorite stories from the gospels, the lives of the saints, or contemporary film or literature? What do these choices tell you about yourself?

- If you could add one story to those described in this chapter, which would it be?

A Catholic Chorus

Zoe: This world traveler visited Spain for her seventy-fifth birthday and has attended mass all over the world. She says:

"Some places have their grand cathedrals, but I'm more moved by the dusty village churches where a chicken or goat wanders through. Once, in Mexico, I kept looking at the seat of my pew. The lady next to me had been so gracious—welcoming me despite limited language. It turned out she'd just been to the butcher. On the seat of the pew was a plastic bag filled with bloody beef bones!"

"When I was growing up in rural Kansas, Lutherans and Methodists had a strong sense of belonging to their church community. But Catholics had belonging on steroids!"

"I noticed it even before I converted: Catholics are more fun. With notable exceptions. . . ."

Chapter 3

The Bold Claims

A STAUNCH STAND ON JUSTICE

Catholic kids are raised with the conviction that they can change the world. It's not a bad outlook to establish early in life, like an encouragement to reach for the skies. Later, we learned that each person would make a unique contribution, depending on gifts, education, and interests. But surely the stance on justice has inspired some of the most remarkable saints, as well as some of the finest anonymous efforts around the world.

One disclaimer: From papal writings to bishops' conferences and individual leaders, the church has a treasure trove of principles and guidelines for work toward justice. Orbis Books has published many excellent books on the subject. Regard this short chapter as merely an introduction to more thorough works.

It begins with the essence of human dignity: we were all created in God's image. Furthermore, God became incarnate in Jesus, further blessing all human flesh. A huge denial of that reality is the way that some peoples are tortured, dehumanized, oppressed, belittled, and deprived of life's essentials. In sweatshops and genocides the treasure of human life is utterly disregarded. The true search for justice tries to eliminate the destructive elements of both wealth and poverty so all can have a dignified life. Whoa—what's destructive about wealth? Loneliness, overmedication, fear, self-indulgence, useless anxiety, and greed are only a few of the problems money can buy. So the #1 goal isn't giving everyone money, but rather developing all humanity to its fullest potential.

Jesus deliberately chose to have "no place to lay his head." Why? And why have countless saints chosen simple lifestyles? Perhaps they knew that the secret of happiness is in relationships, connections, not things. That wisdom is apparent in the following story.

A photographer in Africa watched people in a refugee center lined up to get food. An eight-year old girl was at the end of the line. After four hours, all that was left was a banana. She split it between her younger sister and brother, then licked the peel herself. "The photographer said that generous moment was the first time he accepted the reality of God."[1]

As the story shows, and as St. Vincent de Paul taught: "The poor have much to teach you. You have much to learn from them." Because faith flavors our political action, we are restrained about wanting immediate results. We know we're limited humans who live within the constraints of time. We can exercise only modest control over huge problems like war, world hunger, environmental destruction, and natural disasters.

Institutional giving through parishes and non-profits is generous and necessary. There is an immediate need to finance direct services to the poor—providing food, health care, education, housing, jobs, and so on—while still maintaining their dignity. However, many see just as great a need to change the systems that oppress them. Systemic change encourages the needy to find strategies to help them emerge from poverty. Both are necessary.

A 1971 document from the Synod of Bishops, *Justice in the World*, points out that action for justice and transforming the world is *constitutive* (an absolute requirement) of the church's mission, of any project it undertakes. It also emphasizes an inductive, experiential approach to social problems. Rather than starting with a principle or theory, it looks first to the "cry of the poor." Furthermore, the document recognizes that anyone who attempts to speak about justice must first be just. Hence, the church must examine its own possessions and lifestyle (no. 40).

A long-term investment for justice has been the American Catholic educational system. These schools have educated their communities' children, including rural poor, immigrant families, and minorities such as African Americans and Native Americans.

What heartened us as children continues to inspire—the stories of individuals who changed the segment of their world they could affect. They didn't become overwhelmed by the problems, or "cop out" because of their complexity. For instance, Frederic Ozanam, a husband and father, founded the St. Vincent de Paul Society, which now serves twelve million people a year. In 1848, he wrote with remarkable sensitivity:

> The science of charity reform is not transmitted through books and at assemblies' tribunes as much as by climbing stairs in the home of the poor, kneeling at his bed, suffering from the same cold as he does, and discovering the secret of a grief-stricken heart in the course of a friendly conversation. When we have accomplished this ministry,

---

[1] Tom Fox, "Theology School Founded with a Dream for Asia," *National Catholic Reporter*, April 1, 2011.

not for months, but over long years; when we have thus studied the poor at home, at school, at the hospital, not only in one city but in several, and also in the country, in whatever condition God placed him, then we can start to know the formidable problem of misery, then we are entitled to propose serious measures.

GROUNDED IN IDENTITY

The faith that does justice is grounded in a large and eternal identity. How *else* would we have the chutzpah to approach such huge challenges?

"Who do you think you are?" This question was posed to Jesus by Jews he had annoyed with his apparent arrogance (Jn 8:53). His enemies' instinct was to demonize him, but ironically, they divinize him—and us in turn. This is how Jesus calls us to share his life and freedom. Responding to the call is the most important decision we'll ever make.[2] Taking on human nature, Jesus invited us "to his own glory and excellence," to make us "partakers of the divine nature" (2 Pt 1:3, 4).

When Jesus says, "The Father and I are one" (Jn 10:30), we can say that of ourselves. The bottom-line identity of the human being is "beloved child of God." If we really believed that, wouldn't it make a huge difference? We would no longer plod through our routines, heightened only by the drama of crisis, constantly lugging the baggage of guilt or anxiety. Instead, we would walk freely and joyfully through God's abundance, delighting in God's gifts.

The Jews thought "he was claiming too much for himself." Instead, "he is claiming too much for them." He invites them—and us—to participate in his unfettered, unguarded divinity. "If the Son sets you free, then you will be really free" (Jn 8:36). Later, Jesus refers to Psalm 82:6, "I say, you are gods, children of the Most High, all of you." (10:34) If this sounds too impossible, it's important to qualify. We are freed from worry, not from sadness. He challenges his first listeners to an even greater life than Abraham promised them—but they preferred the familiar, tried-and-true.[3]

Jesus "seems to have been moving messiahship from its projection onto public leaders, however great, to an inner reality whose latent powers everyone must discover for themselves."[4]

---

[2] Demetrius Dumm, *A Mystical Portrait of Jesus* (Collegeville, MN: Liturgical Press, 2001), 139.

[3] Ibid., 137.

[4] Walter Wink, *The Human Being: Jesus and the Enigma of the Son of the Man* (Minneapolis, MN: Fortress Press, 2001), 117.

What Jesus found within, a deep intimacy with his Father, is open to all of us. The power of the Messiah is within our reach—when we teach, heal, or pass on the good news. No one is excluded from God's reign.

This is why, confronting the hunger of the five thousand (Lk 9:12–13), he told the disciples, "*You* give them something to eat." Or why he involved the crowd gathered at Lazarus's tomb: *You* roll away the stone; *you* unbind him (Jn 11:39, 44). Don't expect God to do everything; that's why God gave us power and intelligence.

Shortly after the raising of Lazarus, a rich affirmation of identity poured from the cross when Jesus' arms, nailed to wood, embraced and saved us. As Paul commented, it's hard to believe anyone would sacrifice like this for a virtuous person, but Jesus did so for evil people. "You were worth it," Jesus seems to say.

RESURRECTION TO ETERNAL LIFE

Even the astounding claims to eternal life made at Easter are about us as well as about Jesus. As Garry Wills says, "Jesus was resurrected into us. We walk around living his life after his death. . . . He still slips into, through, and around the structures that would confine and confound him."[5]

Fran Ferder echoes this idea: "In some mysterious way he had risen—risen in their hearts, risen in their lives, and was now closer to them than their heartbeat, nearer than their breath. He lived in them."[6]

Seeing life through the lens of resurrection emphasizes its joys. To be sure, most lives are also filled with dark spaces. But psychologists tell us that where we place the emphasis will determine the quality of life. It's usually not hard to see a difference between people who focus on the unlucky, unhealthy, tragic parts, and those who pour energy and attention into the positives.

"I have seen the Lord," Mary Magdalene told the other disciples, in disarmingly simple words. (This was, after all, the Lord they had seen crucified, then entombed, lifeless.) Later, the other disciples would echo her, telling Thomas who had been absent: "We have seen the Lord" (Jn 20:25). These words become the hallmark of every Christian, as we see Jesus in the circumstances of life, one another, and the beauty of our world. Recognizing even the faintest traces of his face, we rejoice.

Even when we're caught in mysterious suffering, Christ's resurrection gives us grounds for hope. We live "knowing that he who raised Jesus, the

---

[5] *What Jesus Meant* (New York: Viking, 2006), 138.

[6] *Enter the Story* (Maryknoll, NY: Orbis Books, 2010), 147.

Lord, will raise us along with him, and bring us to his side" (2 Cor 4:14). If I'm created by God and belong to God, then what am I so worried about?

THE BUSINESS OF IMPOSSIBILITY

The difficulty? Believing the claims and living up to them. We sometimes seem content with small change, when the essence of the faith offers us thousand dollar bills. John of the Cross seemed to know this when he asked, "Created for such grandeur, what are you doing, O soul?"

Even as small children, Catholics know they're not just on earth for their own pleasure. Always, we are called to something greater; we are noble children of the King. Our gifts are given for the service of Christ's kingdom on earth. No matter how little we think we have, we're taught early on to share that with others.

The claims might seem impossible, if we didn't see them actualized in holy lives.

THE PRIESTHOOD OF THE BAPTIZED

In 1964, Jacques Maritain, an eminent Catholic philosopher, reflected on the lack of joy in the practice of the faith:

> What a pity then that for so long . . . the Christian laity have believed themselves destined to imperfection, to a life of sin redeemed at the end, possibly, by a "happy death." They have cheerfully accepted this criminal dichotomy created by Baroque Catholicism. . . .
>
> If there is a single outstanding responsibility that should weigh upon the clergy of our time, it is to help the faithful escape from the damnable despair caused by this dichotomy and its paralyzing effects upon human history. . . . The faithful [must] become aware of their vocation to share in the holiness of Jesus and his redemptive work.

Shortly after this was written, Vatican II issued the "universal call to holiness," which radically changed the dilemma Maritain describes. It insisted that Christ calls *everyone* to holiness and offers the grace to accomplish sanctity in a rich variety of forms. In contrast to earlier church documents, this one didn't specify rules or condemn bad behavior. Instead, it spoke of God's people in warm terms of dignity, welcome, tenderness, and safe haven.

This shouldn't have come as dramatic news. Father Paul Philibert, OP, writes in *The Priesthood of the Faithful* that from the beginning of time, God has been creating a likeness, a people who would be a moving, active, visible image of God's invisible heart. Because Jesus' heart is God's, and he became human, he has sanctified everything human. Thus, a people become priestly because they are in solidarity with him.

Thus God dwells and acts in human flesh. Everything we do is united to this deepest meaning of human life. The priesthood of the baptized is thus a synergy with the priesthood of Christ.

Fortunately God, unlike the Marines, isn't looking for "a few good men." God draws everyone, many members into the *totus Christus* (complete Christ). And our relationship to God isn't one of slave to master but of beloved child to adoring parent. Philibert calls it the "marvelous bargain." He adds, "We offer our lives in all their concreteness, and God offers us through the gift of the Spirit a share in the passage of Christ from dying to rising."[7]

While there's a difference between the common priesthood of all the baptized and the ministerial priesthood of the ordained, the one Spirit works through both, creating a priestly people. If we have today a sharp division between the ordained and everyone else, it was never intended by Christ, who ordained no one.

Father Philibert believes we've become overly clericalized if we identify "the church's holiness and transformative power with the rites of liturgical celebration and not with the Christian transformation of families, cities, work and culture."[8]

The specific role of lay people is to be light and salt in places where the gospel can be spread only by them. They see that the gospel never detonates under church rafters but only out in the world. The *real* work doesn't get done in the rectories or churches but in offices, factories, shops, and homes of the faithful.

This empowering message may be hard to absorb. Throughout the Bible the message recurs: you are not a slave, but a friend, an adopted child with an eternal inheritance—not condemned to a life of futility and an empty death. Jesus has sanctified everything human, making us indeed a "chosen race, a royal priesthood, a holy nation" (1 Pt 2:9).

The implications could indeed be unsettling. God choose each of us for a unique purpose and equips us to get it done. With the shiny new identity card given us at baptism, we are commissioned for a specific work in the kingdom. Role models are fine, but we need never look too admiringly at anyone else—Oh, *Kelly* is so generous, *Sister Margaret* so holy; the *Campbell family* really has its act together!

---

[7] Paul Philibert, OP, *The Priesthood of the Faithful* (Collegeville, MN: Liturgical Press, 2005), 47.

[8] Ibid., 16.

Indeed, such envy distracts us from our real work, our engagement with the circumstances God has designed for us alone. Many saints weren't missionaries to foreign countries. Instead, they sanctified their own particular family or job, or responded to the aching needs in their own communities.

Jesus corrected Peter after the resurrection when he asked about the Beloved Disciple. "What concern is it of yours?" (Jn 21:22). He meant, Don't hanker for anyone else's life, but focus on your own.

What marvelous assurance—and it's not just bolstering the weak kneed or lily livered. The gospels discourage us from pursuing solely our own preoccupations and making ourselves the center of the universe. They remind us that, first and foremost, we belong to God. "For if we live, we live for the Lord, and if we die, we die for the Lord; so then, whether we live or die, we are the Lord's" (Rom 14:8). Because we stand in solidarity with Christ, our daily activity becomes the stuff of our priesthood.

That could mean something as ordinary as grocery shopping, a phone conversation, a walk in autumn leaves. If we are present to the vast possibilities contained in even routine actions, it's all sacred. That struck me one day as I was preparing to give a talk in a room adjoining the church. This particular presentation was equipment intensive: posters, PowerPoint, props, books, and more. I hurried to ready everything for the audience that would arrive after the mass going on in church. At one point, I heard the pastor say familiar words: "This is my body. This is my blood."

We believe this is a current reality, happening among us now, not in some nostalgic past. As Jeremy Driscoll, OSB, points out, the institution narrative or high point of the mass begins in the past tense. Jesus *took, blessed, broke, gave, said.* Then he shifts to the present tense. Quoting Jesus in the "now" moment, this *is* my body and blood, here for you just as surely as it was for those friends gathered at the Last Supper.[9]

If that consecration doesn't apply to everything, then it applies to nothing: appreciating the plump orange at breakfast, soothing a cranky child, getting to work in all weathers. Spouses, siblings, and friends humor, challenge, and give tenderness to one another. Employees do their jobs, and all this is clothed in the fabric of sacramentality. Central to Catholicism is this idea of sacramentality: the visible signs of what God is doing invisibly in the world.

The Dogmatic Constitution on the Church sums up the roles of ordained and baptized: "As the role of the ordained priest is to consecrate bread and wine to be the Body and Blood of Christ, so the role of the layperson is to consecrate the entire world!" (no. 34).

---

[9] Jeremy Driscoll, OSB, *What Happens at Mass* (Chicago: Liturgy Training Publications, 2005), 89–90.

QUESTIONS FOR REFLECTION OR DISCUSSION

- What seems to get in the way of believing in our marvelous identity?
- Where in an ordinary day could you say, "I have seen the Lord?" Where do you see your priesthood there?
- Reread 1 Corinthians 12 and determine how your particular talents can serve the body of Christ.

A Catholic Chorus

Erin: "When I was eight, my family lived in Peru. We became friendly with the Maryknoll missioners there, and I was so impressed by them. They were there first to help, not to convert." Her insight is borne out by the Maryknoll website: articles about protesting a dam in Chile that would flood over fifteen thousand acres of Patagonian wilderness, hopes to end AIDS by 2020, and a Maryknoll priest in Muslim Bangladesh whose goal is "to make a mark of Christianity, not for the purpose of conversion but simply for the idea of showing what a Christian is and does." Native people who have watched his service to seriously sick people comment: "He said he only came to do good and that is what he does."

Catholic Relief Services, Mercy Corps, and many other Catholic organizations are quick to the scene after a tsunami, earthquake, or other natural disaster. Within the United States, Jesuit, Loretto, Holy Cross, and Vincentian volunteers all work in challenging areas of extreme poverty.

Chapter 4

The Role of Ritual

It happens every year. I show up dutifully to make a retreat without a clue why I'm there. Oh, there's a vague sense that it's good to review one's life annually. I'm drawn to the beauty of the retreat-house grounds, its well-stocked cookie jar, and my wise spiritual director. But the first few, silent, empty hours are hard to fill. Especially for one driven by deadlines, usually racing to cram too much into a day, it's that oxymoron, an abrupt slow down. The novel at the bottom of the suitcase beckons temptingly.

So I do what I've always done: the ritual walk to the gazebo; the checkup on water lilies; filling the coffee mug; making sure the hummingbirds are still circling the fountain in the courtyard; a survey of the schedule, the other retreatants, and the daily menu. And it's all where it belongs: the schedule of liturgies; the roses along the stone wall; the pond; the same soft, clean sheets; the minuscule bar of soap. A certain order must be in place to align a launching pad.

Each year that cycle of revisiting and remembering somehow bridges the awkward transition. Soon I find my favorite chair for cloud gazing, clear a space for yoga, retrace the hiking trail, and open an empty journal. "Let the creative juices flow!" I want to shout, remembering that many articles, poems, and books have been inspired and written here in this broad, welcoming space. Without the usual distractions of cooking, cleaning, laundry, phone, grocery shopping, and other domestic duties, my writing muscles seem to expand and grow wings.

Once I've paced out my "turf," the inner work can begin. My director always starts with the prologue to John's Gospel. "Which lines sing like a hymn through the past year? Where have you encountered the light and the dark?" she asks.

I've kept those lists of light and dark, so it's interesting to compare this year's experiences with the previous year's. Almost always I'm overwhelmed with gratitude: "From his fullness we have all received, grace upon grace" (Jn 1:16). It's also fascinating to study the chiaroscuro, an artist's term for the places that light and dark intermingle on a canvas, like light in a forest, dappled by leaves. For instance, a relative's death in November was sad. But it brought an outpouring of family affection, visits from all my children, and some wonderful meal-time, memory-rich conversations.

The silence that at first seems stilted and unfriendly eventually unfolds as a place to hear important whispers. What have I walled away from consciousness simply because I'm too busy to deal with it? What voice niggles in my life, needing attention before it balloons into a greater problem? Being surrounded by careful people who are doing the same work creates a community beyond small talk. We don't exchange the usual pleasantries because we are all engaged in deeper inner work. It takes all our energy and concentration, it's a high priority, and we have only a few days. Chatter seems irrelevant. Afterward, we may look on these silent companions as friends in a unique sense.

Most important, this is a chance to deepen our friendship with God. The empty time, long walks, liturgies, and opportunities for reflection are designed to enhance an all-important relationship that in the press of busy routines often gets short shrift. The Ignatian ideal of prayer fittingly describes this sacred space: "I am going to prayer. I am going to a personal encounter with my one great love."

If the retreat ritual centers me every year and alerts me to the blessings of the previous year, how much more grounding is the weekly ritual that accomplishes the same thing more often. Catholics who love the church for its ritual must find in it the same rhythmic, familiar roots I discover at the retreat center. The four parts of the Catholic mass, our daily or weekly "premier occasion," correspond to the routine I love there. Furthermore, they are the anchors of a life in which the Eucharist reveals our life's meaning, and we find our life's meaning in Eucharist.

EVERYONE NEEDS AN ENTRANCE RITE

The Entrance Rite refers to an opening hymn, a procession into the church with the presider and altar servers, the lector holding the book of readings, sometimes candles or banners or bells. It draws our attention to something important happening here; we are crossing the threshold into liminal, sacred space. With all our differences, we become one people called here by God, bringing our unique struggles, stories, triumphs, and disappointments.

This part of the mass corresponds to the first hours at the retreat house: slowing down, revisiting familiar paths, bonding silently with other participants, remembering our identity as God's children, starting a life-giving dialogue.

Why Do We Gather Again and Again?

Our gathering at mass begins long before we stand and sing the opening hymn. As Cardinal Roger Mahony explains in "Gather Faithfully Together," his letter to the Archdiocese of Los Angeles, it begins as the alarm clocks ring in homes, apartments, dormitories, and trailer courts all over the parish. The Spirit draws people together from different socioeconomic backgrounds, races, political parties, and age groups. They speak many different native languages and have many concerns on their minds. "The Sunday assembly should bring together men, women and children of all ages. It should be the one experience in our lives when we will not be sorted out by education level, skin color, intelligence, politics, sexual orientation, wealth or lack of it, or any other human condition" (no. 94).

The priest's initial greeting is not the sloppy "Hi," or "How ya doin'?" of a grocery-store exchange. The dignified courtesy of his speech reminds us that the grace and peace of the Trinity abide with us and within us. His gesture is significant; the wide extension of his hands welcomes all into Jesus' inclusive embrace.

As many different people sing or pray together, they become one voice, one people in Christ. All are marked with the sign of the cross, signifying that all belong to Christ. They are precious to the Father, redeemed by the Son, and filled with the grace of the Holy Spirit.

Jesus was not only a historic figure who lived in Palestine under the Roman occupation. He is with us now, offering himself as our food and drink. Knowing how difficult our days can be, he wants to walk through them with us, beside us, within us.

We want to remember Jesus as a living presence among us still—not like the album a mother shows her son so he'll know his deceased father, or the shrine of pictures and mementos the daughter builds for her mother who died last year. Our presence here speaks our belief: Jesus lives now.

Why Do We Cry "Kyrie"?

During this part of the mass we ask for mercy because we know we don't deserve to be here. At the retreat house I'm aware of many people who certainly merit the opportunity but don't have the time or money to get away as I do. At mass, we know that such scruffy, insecure, rambunctious, and sinful sorts as we have no business invoking the most high God. The church asks for mercy at this time because we always come tarnished to this celebration. No matter how spiffy our clothes or how sterling our intentions, we must mourn our losses and clean up our act before we approach this feast:

- We have fallen far short of our ideals.
- We have betrayed our dearest loves.
- We have squandered God's abundant gifts.
- We have lost our friends and not fulfilled our bright potential.
- We have let beauty pass unnoticed and focused on ugliness.
- We have forgotten what is important and remembered what is trivial.
- We are filled with anger, jealousy, frustration.
- By our silence we have enabled oppressive systems.
- By our inaction we have allowed the vulnerable to be hurt.
- We have let fear dominate our personal and public lives.
- We have blamed evil on everyone else.

Limping and brokenhearted, we do not know where to turn. We can only ask for mercy. We can ask it only from Jesus, who wept, who agonized, who knew directly the pain of human loss.

Throughout Eastern and Western liturgies the call resounds: *Kyrie, eleison. Christe, eleison. Kyrie, eleison.* The sung melody can be haunting; the Greek words have been on the lips of Christians for centuries.

A Time to Praise

And then, as if we've cleared the air, we sing "Gloria," just as Mary and Elizabeth did under difficult circumstances. One woman was unmarried and pregnant, the other old and pregnant. The most natural thing in the world would have been to grouse about their nausea or aching backs over the picket fence. They had plenty of unfairness to complain about! Instead, they praise. We follow their lead.

Henri Nouwen suggests that four words in the institution narrative are key to the eucharistic ritual: *taken, blessed, broken,* and *given.*[1] The word that summarizes the Entrance Rite is *taken*. Flawed as we are, we are lucky to be here, chosen and lifted into the hands of Christ.

Just as I enter the mass or retreat space, so I need to enter my daily life. How often do I go through the motions thoughtlessly? I take for granted the clean water, the food in the pantry, the people who are kind even before caffeine. I notice my car only when it doesn't start, or an efficient road system only when it's clogged with snow. In my dash to work or the gym, I rarely give thanks for the legs that carry me or the health that sustains me. Chatting with friends or relatives, I often keep an eye on my watch, rarely pausing to think how much these people mean to me. Central heat, computers, dishwashers, and electricity are blessings much of the world aches to have. If I collapsed suddenly, an ambulance would whisk me off to

---

[1] Henri Nouwen, *Life of the Beloved* (New York: Crossroad, 2002).

competent health care. Should I need more books, I can request them from home through a free, easily accessible library. This brief litany is only the beginning—each person could compose his or her own. The Entrance Rite helps me see my blessings more thoughtfully, appreciate them more often.

LIFE THROUGH A SACRED LENS—THE LITURGY OF THE WORD

My retreat director often invites me to dialogue with a "wisdom figure." While this might be a relative, a friend, or an author, it's often a scriptural character. Over the years I've gotten chummy with the woman at the well, Peter, the woman who anointed Jesus, the Beloved Disciple, Nicodemus, and Martha. These feisty characters invite us to know them better and relate their lives to ours. Imaginatively placing ourselves in the gospel story, writing a letter to, or imagining a dialogue with a character are all techniques used to reduce our distance from these ancient texts and make them stories that resonate within us.

Through the Readings we learn week after week to interpret life in terms of scripture and symbol. When we're tempted to lambast a coworker or despair of a spouse or child, the parable of weeds and wheat encourages us to hold off, restrain our anger, and not treat the world violently. (The farmer refuses to yank the weeds, hard to distinguish from the crop, but allows them to grow together with the wheat.) If God sees this world with kindness (even a sinful place like Nineveh), how can we treat it angrily? If God restrains rage, which must be the natural response to our wasteful, greedy ways, who are we to hurl venom at supposed offenders?

Or we read the parable of the lost coin (Lk 15:8–10). In it a woman lights a lamp and sweeps the house, searching for her lost coin. Upon finding it, she rejoices with her friends and neighbors. Father Michael Joncas once enriched that parable in a talk, explaining that the coins represented a woman's dowry, tied up in her hair at a time before banks or social security. The dirt floor was covered with woven reed mats, resembling tatamis. On it fell garbage; through it scurried vermin. She must muck through it, just as God must scramble thorough the refuse, hunting for us. God in this parable isn't some distant potentate, but intimately involved, even throwing a party when we are found. And at some level, we are already found, redeemed by Christ.

We who lose small things like glasses, paperwork, and keys know the joy of finding them; how much more thrilling it must be when God's beloved child finds an identity and a future again. We hear the same stories over and over, but we are different people. One week we hear it differently from another week, notice another detail, respond to messages and words at various levels. It's like reading a good book; the text is the same, but we read it differently at age twenty, forty, and sixty.

The messages of scripture give us a way to pattern our experience. Jesus said, "If you abide in me, and my words abide in you, ask for whatever you wish, and it will be done for you" (Jn 15:7). Indeed, the word is a spacious home filled with messages of courage, conviction, freedom. If we live there, we need never be threatened by the doomsayers, negative voices, those who discount our marvelous heritage. Scripture may challenge, but it always assures us that we are beloved children of God. Our future is filled with hope. What more do we need to know?

The key word for this section is *blessed.* According to Nouwen, "A blessing touches the original goodness of the other and calls forth his or her Belovedness."[2] This doesn't mean that we ignore the world's evil. Instead, scripture strengthens us to live under the blessing rather than the curse.

LITURGY OF THE EUCHARIST

That bottom-line conviction of identity is given tangible form in the bread and wine, our gifts transformed into Christ's body and blood. We call down God's Spirit upon those gifts and plunge ourselves into them, finding there the ultimate meaning of our lives. Just as wheat and grapes are the work of bakers and growers, transformed into bread and wine, so we too offer the ordinary stuff of our lives to be consecrated into Jesus, who comes into our midst again and again and again.

Jesus upset the social hierarchies of his day, with their firm rules about who ate together, who sat where, and who ate what. Throughout his life, through word and behavior, Jesus insisted that food taboos were meaningless. The natural bounty of creation was to be eaten and celebrated, not parceled out according to merit. As Nathan Mitchell points out, he subverted all the power-hungry, dominating strategies that look out primarily for #1.[3]

It's poignant that Jesus, who must've lived fully in the present, gives the Eucharist the night before he is chillingly betrayed and brutally tortured. Because he is so joyful even then, looking forward to the Passover meal, and so inclusive, Jesus set the bar high: all Christians should practice radical hospitality. The bread he broke would foretell his body broken for us. How then can we condemn one another?

At the retreat house I see experiences in retrospect. Often they take on a meaning they lacked in immediacy. As I review the year since my last retreat, I ask, "Where was God in all this?" The answer may not always be clear, but glimmers appear that weren't there before. What at first seemed like a disaster may have turned into a gift. Early signals aren't always the

---

[2] Ibid., 56.

[3] *Real Presence: The Work of Eucharist* (Chicago: Liturgy Training Publications, 2007).

most accurate ones. A person I at first thought strange has become a friend. Breaking open the bread of our lives, we find nurture there.

We live in a society where much is broken: the economy, the ecology, the fragile peace among nations, the inner peace of relationships. Only to close friends do we reveal our own vulnerability—though sometimes we don't want to admit it even to ourselves! Yet this part of the Eucharist demonstrates clearly that denial seldom works to heal pain. What seems more effective is naming and embracing it because it has much to teach us. The word for this section is *broken.*

Seeing pain as proof of our worthlessness only worsens it. Seeing it as meant to deepen and enrich our belovedness makes it bearable. What Jesus did at the Last Supper is still a mystery, but it points in the direction of turning harsh suffering into food for ourselves and others. His metaphor is still apt today: a woman enduring childbirth soon forgets her suffering in her joy that a person has been born (Jn 16:21). We too can learn that sometimes pain signals a radical new beginning, the start of new life.

COMMUNION WITH THE HOLY

What is life all about if not communion with the holy? An annual retreat is a way to connect with what is most important in life, often glazed over in busyness. Simply by slowing down, I can look more appreciatively at the realities there (the lily pond, the soaring hawks) and at all the realities that constitute my life. All make up the unique text that God is writing there, my story, one unlike anyone else's story.

When I think of the people I most admire, they have drawn grace and courage from their relationship with God. This deep well is their inner source; it sustains them through loss, disappointment, and tragedy. The future often looks scary; we wonder sometimes how we'll even get through the day. The Eucharist is a visible sign that we do not walk forward alone. Over and over, Jesus gives himself as bread and wine, through us. We then become bread and cup for one another.

Father Vince Hovley, SJ, points out that white light pouring through a crystal becomes little rainbows sparkling around a room. Our ordinary lives, shining through the prism of the Eucharist, make the most ordinary experiences into meetings with the sacred. To live in communion with the holy dispels aloneness, strengthens us, and sends us forth to a hurting, hungry world.

Many of those interviewed for "A Catholic Chorus" named the ritual as their favorite part of being Catholic. If our Eucharist is our primary ritual, from which all else flows, it indeed gives meaning to our lives. Furthermore, it gives us courage to move forward. The word for this section is *given.* After we are chosen, blessed, and broken, we are given.

The Catholic church doesn't exist for the sake of its lovely liturgies, choirs, or stained glass. Instead, it impels us to go forth to a hurting, hungry world, where we do what we can.

Many more chapters could be written about the smaller things that compose the ritual, but for now I'll mention only one: candles. Those silent, glowing vessels for light have their own eloquent speech. When the seven French Trappists of Algeria mentioned in Chapter 2 were kidnapped in 1996, seven candles were lit on the altar of Notre Dame Cathedral to represent hope that they were alive. When word came of their death, these were snuffed out. But for the funeral service the candles were relighted, a symbol that their lives had become eternal. Or, in the words of the Trappist abbot general, Father Bernardo Olivera, at the funeral, "A life freely given in the spirit of love is never a life lost, but one found again in Him who is Life."[4]

QUESTIONS FOR REFLECTION OR DISCUSSION

- Do you have daily rituals, not necessarily related to church, that ground your day? If so, describe them.
- What does it mean to you to pass through the doorway of the church? Can you enter with the same reverence into your own experience of work, play, the presence of others? Why or why not?
- The Bishops' Committee on Divine Worship says, "The people of God . . . form a society whose task it is to praise." Have you ever thought of your "job description" that way? Why or why not?
- What is your favorite bible story? What does your choice tell you about yourself?
- In the Eucharist the ordinary becomes extraordinary. How does that continue after we leave the church?

A Catholic Chorus

Lily: A financial professional, Lily is also a wife and mom. She says, "I like the balance of the liturgy. At the Presbyterian church I just get talked at. I also like the saints who inspire us, and the religious orders like a fraternity or sorority—you can hang out with your own kind of folks! Anywhere in the world I go to mass, I get it. The layering of culture on the mass makes it the same but different. I love Lent—as a community we go within ourselves in a more meaningful, directed way than the rest of the year."

[4] Quoted in John W. Kiser, *The Monks of Tibhirine* (New York: St. Martin's Press, 2002), 4.

Chapter 5

The Words We Treasure

It was a rainy night, and I couldn't sleep. But nothing comforts more than reading a good book accompanied by the wash of rain. Geraldine Brooks is one of my favorite authors, and suddenly at 2 a.m., I was hooting aloud with recognition. I hadn't known she was once Catholic until I read this passage:

> At the age of ten, I decked my room with the gory paraphernalia of Catholicism. An anatomically correct crucified Christ writhed over the dresser, a Sacred Heart dripped blood by the door. My brain itched with the abstract thought required by the Sacred Mysteries. Three persons, one God. And the Word was made flesh. I loved the potent metaphor of the litany of Mary: Lily of the Valley, Mystic Rose, Star of the Sea.[1]

To which I could add: May crowning. Mysteries of the Rosary. Pagan babies. Vatican City. Lourdes. "Offer it up." Confirmation name. While some of those may be dated, some still remain: "The Lord be with you," RCIA, triduum, O Antiphons, epiclesis, Guadalupe.

For a sensitive child or adult, it's a nourishing soup. What makes it so intriguing is that it hovers on some murky borderland between the black-and-white clarities of earthly life and the mysterious suggestions of another life, wafting within range but still beyond our grasp. In one line poet Brian Doyle captured a gesture so common to Catholics (and perhaps other pew folk) that few ever notice: "The slight polite hesitation as someone looks to lift the kneeler."[2]

While we might be firmly planted in Iowa or the Australian outback, we remain the imaginatively wandering citizens of the vast Catholic world: Monte Casino. San Salvador. Knock shrine in Ireland. Walsingham.

---

1 Geraldine Brooks, *Foreign Correspondence* (New York: Doubleday, 1998), 29.

2 "Easter," *America* (May 2–9, 2011), 20.

Medjugorje. Christ's statue overlooking the harbor of Rio de Janeiro. Such lingo eludes definition or reduction. Even an explanation doesn't do it complete justice. Maybe as children we just liked to roll those mysteries around on our tongues, knowing we belonged to a bigger family, a larger circle defying time and space, a vaster identity.

The "code" is hard to describe, and probably every religion has a collection of quirky abbreviations, gestures, and phrases that only the "in" crowd knows—or cares about. Just as each profession has its jargon, so each religious tradition has its lingo. Certainly not doctrine, theology, or matters of substance, these are more the fun fluff, often the subject of jokes and laughter rather than issues inspiring belief. Others hear something so inexplicable and smile distantly, fairly sure they've uncovered a pocket of craziness better left buried.

It explains why in certain cities the question, "Where did you go to high school?" if answered, "St. Mary's," "St. Joe's," or "Regis," will uncover a bond of shared experience and background that stupefies the uninitiated. Unless, of course, the two in the conversation attended schools with *rival* sports teams, which resulted in hilarious headlines such as "Sacred Heart Trounces Blessed Mother," "Annunciation Kills St. Mark's," and so on. In other cities the first question is, "What parish are you from?" This seemingly innocuous question unlocks an avalanche of shared experience, often starting with the inspiring (or crazy) pastor.

Only examples and stories can explore this bit of Catholicism, and even they may not clarify the muddy waters of the code. I encountered it again recently. In a strange city with an unfamiliar language, I attended a Catholic church. Over the doorway was marked this cryptic message: 20 C + M + B 11. Understanding little of the service, I knew immediately what that meant. On the feast of the Epiphany, shortly after Christmas, marking the visit of the magi to the infant Jesus, the Catholic custom is to bless the house and mark the doorway with that formula: the first two digits of the current year on the left and the last two on the right, bracketing the initials of the legendary three kings: Caspar, Melchior, and Balthasar.

Sister Kate Dooley once had an audience at the Chicago Catechetical Conference laughing at her story of "the clicker." Veterans of Catholic schools "back in the day" will recognize the clicker—a small wooden device that made a sound out of all proportion to its size. Even inexperienced young sisters wielding one could bring a crowd of three hundred kids to their knees: one click, one knee; two clicks, both knees. I suspect that when an untrained teacher wasn't sure what to do with an unruly class, she fingered the secret weapon in her pocket. The clicker could halt stampeding hordes! Such unquestioned power in "old time" religion!

Many years later, Sister Kate said, she wandered into a Washington DC nature store. A couple was delighting in their discovery of clickers shaped like frogs, with beady eyes and body painted on the wooden frame. "Remember *these*?" the woman chortled, merrily clicking away. Her husband immediately genuflected.

Another couple joined them, apparently from the same distinguished company: survivors of Catholic schools. They were strangers but instantly began exchanging memories and making plans to buy frog clickers. Then they saw Sister Kate, who probably hasn't worn a habit in thirty years, and asked, "Don't you want to buy one too?"

"Thanks," she smiled. "I still have mine."

One lady rushed into apology. "Oh, sister, I'm so sorry! Some of my mother's best friends are nuns! She still sends them Christmas cards." Nothing like the presence of a "nunny" authority figure to turn competent adults into babbling children.

Certain Catholic feasts evoke lyrical writing, like Brian Doyle's description of All Souls' Day: "The most honest Christian day of them all . . . All Souls Day is exactly that, all of us day, all the frightened and broken and bruised and weary us day, the day we hold hands and admit we are muddled but alive with hope, riveted by love, suffused with light, though our eyes be blinded sometimes . . . ; the day we pause and consider the road ahead, filled with dirty dishes and tiny connivances and larger lies, and remember that we are graced by billions of teammates . . . also on the muddy road toward His embrace."[3]

From the sublime to the ridiculous: Hot debate of "the rules" can also forge instant bonds. One woman proudly announced that she'd bought her stash of chocolate candy to plunge into as Lent ended. (Catholic kids were encouraged to "give something up" for Lent. We usually forfeited some treat like candy.) "Yup," this seventy-something gloated. "I'm ready to dig in on Easter Sunday."

"No!" howled a chorus of people who had also endured childhood Lents. "It's noon on Holy Saturday! We remember watching the clock!"

The first woman was distraught. "You mean all those years, I waited an extra *day*?" It was enough to make her plant her face in chocolate three weeks early to compensate for all those years of deprivation.

When a moviemaker wants to show religion, it's usually Catholic, probably because it's so easy to demonstrate with outward signs: vestments, statues of Mary, the sign of the cross, a chalice. A local theater producer who had staged "Nunsense" said it was easy to identify the Catholics in the audience; they were laughing the most and got all the jokes.

---

[3] "All of Us Day," *Give Us This Day*, vol. 1, no. 4 (November 2011), 6.

A convert to Catholicism after her marriage, one woman felt befuddled by all the code there was to learn. She thought she'd never get it, fervently hoping, "Just don't throw a novena at me!" But a dear priest consoled her, "You don't have to buy it all."

So when we see Hemmingway's *Moveable Feast,* we know what the name means. It suggests a fine flexibility, when most feasts are firmly lodged on the calendar. Some, however, can move, depending on the date of Easter, itself moveable. Hemingway borrowed the term for his time in Paris during the 1920s: "If you are lucky enough to have lived in Paris as a young man, then wherever you go for the rest of your life, it stays with you, for Paris is a moveable feast."

Or if Yeats says that a friend whose work has come to nothing is "Bred to a harder thing/Than Triumph," we know that Catholics, while not necessarily scorning success, have at the very least a plausible rationale for suffering. From the first scraped knee in preschool, we learned that our pain is part of Christ's and redeems the world. That may be hard to remember when the migraine is seething or one's love has died.

QUESTIONS FOR DISCUSSION OR REFLECTION

- Have you thought about Catholicism as a link to a larger world? What dimension does this add to the faith?
- Do you treasure any favorite words connected with Catholicism that weren't mentioned here? What are they?

A Catholic Chorus

Paul: The retired chair of a university theology department, Paul is an ardent advocate of Vatican II, husband, father, long-term participant in Jewish-Christian dialogue, author, and editor active in a variety of causes. He says confidently, "There's too much richness in Catholicism to be narrowly focused on the clerical mindset or the hierarchs. The church is so much more than its structures. We can use them where they help, but they're not the total picture. Reality outruns the structures, which will eventually catch up."

He offers the American nuns as an example. He refers to an investigation launched by the Vatican that seems to have generated primarily an outpouring of widespread support. "They didn't let institutional interference stop them from being good Catholics, following their consciences. It was a stance of more than 'grin and bear it.' They simply didn't make it their focus. They engaged the bishops in courteous dialogue but were selective about where to pay attention—or not.

"The sacramental imagination may be overly stressed, but it's vital to Catholicism, which names it in a way other traditions don't. In short, God reaches us—and we reach God—through ordinary concrete realities. For instance, we relax blissfully into bed at night, have an intimate conversation over a glass of wine, or light a candle for a hushed moment of quiet. While others would see these as important, we name them sacred. Such precious times are nothing less than a meeting with God.

"Throughout our tradition Catholics have had a rich sense of the universe as crowded with sacred presence. Through creation and the incarnation, God embraced our world. So at their best, Catholics don't fear or condemn the culture. The human—its science, reasoning, and art—is the body of Christ. So it's not sinful per se. If it's human, it's God's creation, to be appropriated by the church.

"History has fine examples of that embracing attitude. When Germanic tribes used a fir tree as a phallic symbol, Christians didn't simply chop it down. They associated it with the birth of Christ, decorated it, and created the Christmas tree. Similarly, pagan worship of the goddess Isis holding her baby Horus in the late fourth century was enfolded into Catholic reverence for Mary when they converted."

Because Paul is an expert on the far-sighted author William Lynch, SJ, he cites Lynch's focus on irony as a central form of faith. Neither sarcasm nor contempt, it instead springs from the incarnation, God's great ironic joke. It is a saving irony that Absolute Beauty and Power took on the frail and fallible form of a baby, who was eventually executed as a criminal by the state.

That irony helps us laugh at all our own pretensions. It destroys our dreams of perfection, even of the church as perfect. The deepest faith is to know one's self and one's church as sinful, poor, limited, and mortal. And in these realities, we find God's presence. Recognizing our own vulnerability and mortality is immensely freeing. In our very imperfection, God saves us. And thus we allow God to be God.

Many classics tell of a great person failing, and thereby touching grace. Arrogant and superior in their "perfect" state, they became far more compassionate and active for suffering humanity in their "fallen" state.

The insight is supported by scripture. After Jesus' resurrection he could have healed his wounds. Instead, he had Thomas touch them and the places where the nail marks probed. These were the site of mystery and wonder, the locus of divinity.

Chapter 6

So Many "Bests"

Sometimes I'll lean back into an experience, put up my feet and sigh, "This is the best of being Catholic." Then along comes another experience when I think the same thing. A few examples follow.

SISTER GRANDMA

It all began over forty years ago, when after service as a Papal Volunteer in Belize, I knew I couldn't return to start the graduate program at University of Chicago as I'd planned. After a year of living with poverty, I needed a more gradual transition back to the wealthy United States. Fortunately, my aunt, a Victory Noll sister, ran a center in one of Denver's worst neighborhoods. Lyndon Johnson's War on Poverty had provided funding for a summer program for children, which my cousin and I offered to direct. It was a match made in heaven.

Our aunt and her community happily introduced us to the neighborhood, the local attractions, and best of all, the mountains. Although they worked daily with grindingly difficult situations, violent gangs, drug and alcohol addictions and suffering people, they were a remarkably cheerful and upbeat bunch, celebrating everyday miracles. Dinners with them were always fun, the table often decorated, and usually followed by dessert. Perhaps because they'd given me such a warm welcome, or because I loved the mountains so much, I stayed in Denver, completed graduate work, and married.

Some eight years later our oldest son was feeling his lack of grandparents. His only living grandfather was in another city, but his sister, my aunt, had always been a joyful presence in his life. He approached her shyly: "Would you be my foster grandma?" She was delighted and scooped the kindergartner into her arms. "Of course! I'd be thrilled!"

The other children quickly assumed that my aunt was Granny; it didn't bother them that she was also Sister. One day they were leaving her office as a client entered. "Bye, Granny!" each called sweetly. She apologized for the interruption to the woman who said graciously, "Oh, Sister, you be with your grandchildren!" Over thirty years later, slight embarrassment crosses my aunt's face as she tells the story. "She didn't quite get the concept of nuns. So I told her this was my *niece* and her children before any rumors could get started."

Granny had a knack for gifts and notes on each child's birthday; candy for the "major religious feasts," which included Halloween, St. Patrick's Day, and Easter; and root beer floats. "Royalty were never treated as well; no child was ever cherished as much as we were," one daughter remembers. Faithfully, despite blizzards, she'd attend first communions, confirmations, and graduations. Now engaged in their own work with non-profits, the children see her as a model of how to live with compassion and treat all people with a profound and gentle respect. From her they learned that justice is about making love tangible in ways large and small.

Fast-forward to Granny's ninety-eighth birthday. For the event, several of us traveled to the motherhouse in Indiana where she'd retired with many of her friends. Even in old age they were still remarkably gracious women. Within minutes of our arrival, a cart appeared with sandwich fixings, cold drinks, and beer. (They'd never been overly pious, these veterans of tough missions.) One sister spoke fondly of her work with H'mong refugees, who in gratitude had given her a H'mong name that translated to Sister Umbrella. The umbrella not only symbolized their new life in the United States, but also her kind protection, shelter in a strange place.

My aunt was almost totally deaf, but she didn't let that isolate her. At the slightest provocation she'd launch into hysterical stories, like her puzzlement when a poor family in San Antonio had gratefully brought the sisters a live chicken. Or the time the bishop, thrilled with his new television, invited the sisters to share the wealth. Unfortunately, their little town didn't yet have a channel, so they tried to sit appreciatively through snow on the screen and static in the air. Later, when he'd watch his cowboy shows upstairs, her job was distracting visitors for an hour, trying to convince them he was praying, and disguising the thrumming of horse hooves overhead.

A frequent refrain when she described her many kinds of service: "It was such a privilege." Never a complaint, when there must have been plenty of irritations, frustrations, and tragedies. She quoted a hymn that fit her perfectly: "What more could Jesus do?" Many of her friends had died, but she reveled in the present moment. Even in her walker, she gave us a tour that exhausted the young folk, and she made sure we had our afternoon snack of cookies and Cokes. Bent over with osteoporosis, she nevertheless bent even further to touch the arm of a sister whose mind was fine but whose body was almost paralyzed. As she made a date for a chat later, she was the portrait of compassion.

The large campus that the sisters run is noted for its hospitality. In cooperation with Lutheran Services, they offer retreats for women veterans returning from deployment. How peaceful it must be, I thought, after Iraq or Afghanistan: these gardens, beehives, ponds, and grasslands. Each sister, living or dead, has a tree with her name hanging on a small plaque on the trunk. For Arbor Day, local schoolchildren identify the wide variety of trees, hike through areas set aside for conservation, and take home their own sapling. The labyrinth is open to all, and many have entered this form of moving meditation that dates back to medieval cathedrals. The morning I walked it, grass, leaves, and pine needles were gleaming with tiny drops from a recent rain. Each branch, each step bejeweled. It must have been an image for the life of grace, the kind of lives these sisters have so gratefully embraced.

To look back over ninety-eight years with obvious joy and appreciation must be a great gift. Always the Irish storyteller with perfect timing and cadence, Granny loved to embellish precious memories and entertain a new, youthful audience. She even bragged about the Babe Ruth autograph she'd gotten on a baseball by waiting outside the ballpark as a girl. But the story she told most proudly was of a small, shy boy, asking her to be his grandma. Now thirty-seven, he got misty eyed, as did his wife, who was hearing the story for the first time. How appropriate that their first child is due to be born on Granny's ninety-ninth birthday.

A RETREAT

No, *this*, I thought, is the best. God's abundance surrounded us. At a retreat house in the Colorado Rockies, peaks soared, streams gushed, June columbine and lilacs bloomed. That was only the setting. Add in marvelous participants and faculty and staff from Jesuit colleges all over the country, gathered to learn more about Ignatian spirituality.

This, I thought, is the best. Several factors combined to make it a peak experience, aside from the obvious pun.

Setting: We were housed at a retreat house high in the Rocky Mountains. On every side, peaks leap-frogged to stupendous heights. Run-off fresh from glacial snowfields coursed through a river roaring on the grounds. Its music underlay our conversations and soothed our sleep. For a field trip halfway through the week, we explored a national park filled with alpine meadows, deer, picnic sites, hiking trails, and an eight-point elk who nestled majestically beside a gigantic rock where we held spiritual direction.

Participants: As one priest put it, "What better work could there be than accompanying lovers, people who want to learn to love better?" Busy people who take a week away from the rigorous schedule to deepen the quality of their lives tend to be serious, creative, and attentive to what matters. That doesn't mean they're boring. Many wrestle with disillusionment, school budget cuts, the stress of overwork, and personal issues. Several agnostics and a Hindu were among the group's most eloquent, insightful members.

Stimulation: Two talks a day explored Ignatian spirituality, surely one of the healthiest, most realistic approaches to a practical, lived faith. To some extent we all believed—or wanted to—that heartening Ignatian insight: God has a dream for you. Each speaker gave his or her topic a unique spin—from the Jesuit who drew on fifty years' experience living the *Ignatian Exercises* to a mom who described her breast cancer as a participation in the passion of Jesus. When the initial pathology report was grim, she concluded, "I'd let them cut off every body part I had if I could see my nine-year-old daughter graduate from high school, go to college, maybe marry and have a child." A dad related his parenting to Christ's suffering and death. "If God had a daughter . . . ," he speculated, then told of his anguish watching his tiny daughter, born two months early, undergo painful medical procedures. His son, a hard-drinking and partying boy, had subjected his parents to a brutal ten years of wondering whether he was driving drunk, bailing him out of jail, and trudging to court again.

The insights were original and thought provoking. A sample: "When faced with a decision, pray until you are choosing among goods, then choose the greater good." And "God suffuses the world with affection."

A JUBILEE CELEBRATION

No, *this*, I thought, is the best. It was a fiftieth jubilee celebration for Hugh, a priest who represented the finest of that beleaguered institution. A Chicago boy, his speech was still permeated with *dems* and *dese* and *dose,* despite multiple higher degrees, extensive travel, and fluency in several languages.

During his homily, Hugh told us with a kind of boyish wonder how in 1966 he'd been teaching the *Catechism*—in Latin—at a seminary. Then the fresh air of Vatican II swept through the church, and his superior asked if he'd like to study theology. "Sure," he said, and off he went to Switzerland, caught up in heady waves of creativity, pursuing his doctorate with enthusiasm. "What a graced moment that was!" he reminisced.

Other assignments had led him to France, China, Guatemala, Taiwan, and Africa. Without a trace of pride in his accomplishments, Hugh told a self-deprecating story about his time directing a major seminary in a city where the bishop questioned their teaching the more creative theologians like Rahner and Schillebeeckx. After a tense meeting, the group adjourned for a late dinner.

On the way home someone mentioned that they needed a mission statement the next morning, and *he* should write it. "But I can't; I've been drinking!" Hugh protested. Nevertheless, he was stuck with the job and worked on the statement till 2 a.m. The next morning it was quickly accepted with only one word changed. "And that, my friends," Hugh smiled, "is the power of alcohol!"

His mass of celebration was filled with gratitude for his fifty years, for the people there, for all the support and friendship that had filled his days. Songs of calling and response felt so appropriate; this man had lived out his beliefs in abundant divine love and our small, impossible, human efforts to repay.

A COMMUNITY OF WRITERS

Any group that bands together to endure hardship has an easier go of it. While medical, athletic, and military units get more press, an unofficial group without slogans, logos, t-shirts, or any identification papers brings the same comfort and cheer: Catholic writers. Just as only those who are enduring an addiction know how rough it can be, this crew can commiserate. Ridiculous censorship, dwindling budgets, idiot editors, impossible deadlines, incompetent publishers, pathetic pay, angry readers: we've seen it all.

But the bright light is reading a friend's book or article, grinning with appreciation and contacting the person to send compliments. We're not highly competitive—it's a small lift we give each other. And when we appear together in the same issue of a magazine or newspaper, it's friendly to "rub elbows" in print. Once again, different unique voices make up the Catholic chorus.

A recent example is *Give Us This Day,* a monthly publication by Liturgical Press that combines morning and evening prayer, the daily scripture readings, information on the day's saint, and a reflection, usually on the gospel. When first asked to contribute, I stifled a yawn. Similar publications were already on the market, most of them floundering. *Deja vu* all over again.

Then I read the first issue. The publisher had assembled a sterling advisory board and some of the most creative writers active today. Each entry was a jewel that I'd look forward to praying daily. Even for scripture readings that had grown stale with overfamiliarity, a variety of contemporary authors (and some voices from the tradition, like Evelyn Underhill, Monika Hellwig, Henri Nouwen, Teresa of Calcutta, St. John Chrysostom, and St. Thérèse of Lisieux) brought fresh insights.

Happily, people responded. The editor reported a flood of calls and subscriptions, commenting: "People are not only subscribing but telling us how grateful they are for what we are doing. One woman paid for her subscription back in March, and after receiving her first issue she sent a check for twenty-five dollars to help us 'keep up the great work.'"

So much for Catholic apathy. This pocket-sized inspiration proves that people *will* respond to quality; other publications fail because folks are tired of the same old sanitized drek. One example proves how ordinary daily experience bridges us to ineffable light. Editor Mary Stommes in the August 2010 issue wrote of growing up with fourteen siblings and one TV, with one chair and a couch in front of it. Seating space was limited so any child leaving the room had to hold onto territory with an elaborate system of signals, including the words "place saved." This was complicated by more formulas: "Place saved, really saved, and no unsaved."

Anyone who had siblings or offspring nodded in recognition. Then, as I'd hoped she would, Mary developed a parallel to the gospel and concluded with the same metaphor. That skill brings joy to the heart of a writing teacher: we've "come to know a God who saves us in Christ—Christ who bore the weight of our sins on the cross, sits at the right hand of God, saves our place, and wills that there be no unsaved."

I read the meditation aloud to an old friend who had grown up with a punitive, rule-oriented Catholicism. "Ah," he smiled. "What a difference it would've made to think of Jesus saving us a place." Anyone who's entered a crowded bus, cafeteria, or auditorium knows the first pang of bewilderment, then reassurance at the sight of a friend. Even better is the friend's hand on a nearby seat, a nod of "this one's saved for you."

Pushing the metaphor even further, through the Catholic communion of saints, there's wonderful company in the surrounding seats. We may not see them, but we know they're there: Mary Magdalene, Thomas Merton, Teresa of Avila, Thomas More, Cardinal Newman, Mozart, Catherine of Siena, Caryll Houselander, Ignatius of Loyola, Beethoven, Edith Stein, Sts. Francis and Clare, Rembrandt, Leonardo da Vinci, Louis Pasteur, Brahms, Dorothy Day. On a rough day of writer's block, it's nice to imagine them all holding out their hands, jostling for space around an empty chair, signaling "it's yours."

Some of us make our writing more realistic by staying in contact with the people it's designed to touch through the speaker circuit. Usually this means an intense, brief time with a dedicated group of people who never fail to amaze with the depth of their experience and the wisdom of their ideas. The workshop or retreat creates a warm camaraderie, and sometimes long-lasting friendships.

Only with such sympathetic friends could I share a poem like this:

The Writer's Life: An Apology

"Tight deadline," I broadcast,
excusing rude brusqueness
even to the beloved, who
wait helpless for the tempest
to taper. "High dudgeon" a nifty
phrase, unfortunately fitting.

My "break" from "work" a yoga class.
Sailing into the air-conditioned club,
I see a maid sweating in sun,
collecting towels and trash by the pool.
The ancients called it "metanoia," this
sickening twist, this embarrassing self.

QUESTIONS FOR REFLECTION OR DISCUSSION

- Name your three "best" religious experiences over the last year.
- Do you have a support group with whom to share trials, laughter, tribulation, and merriment? Do you think it helps offset stress? Why or why not?

A Catholic Chorus

Jimi: He holds a doctorate in theology from Notre Dame and teaches at a Jesuit university. He and his wife, a pediatrician, have four children, two of them adopted Haitian orphans. His book on Merton is splendid, and he writes of Catholicism with earthy relish: "Tonight we go to our parish festival. I'm dealing Blackjack for the Lord. Free beer and house rules guarantee a big haul for the church. Gotta love these sacred Catholic rituals!"

Chapter 7

The Best-Kept Secrets

Some of the most empowering Catholic beliefs aren't widely known. Yet they demonstrate such respect for the individual, they inspire confidence. Those interested in pursuing more should seek a more scholarly treatment; this chapter serves only as an introduction. Those discussed here are the "ladder" of truths, the *sensus fidelium,* primacy of conscience and internal forum.

THE LADDER OF TRUTHS

At first Catholic doctrines may seem to make up an overwhelming list. But only a few are essential to faith. Not all doctrines are equally important. At the top of the doctrinal hierarchy are revealed truths about God, known only with God's help, for example, the Trinity, the incarnation, the resurrection. These are called *de fide* (of the faith) and are included in the Creed. The "highest degree of certainty" applies to these.

One example from the Jewish tradition: The Ten Commandments were highly revered in scripture as God's direct words, a respect carried on by Christians. Other teachings—on diet, for example—were secondary and not continued by early Christians. Ideas about belief were less important to those first disciples than questions of worship and life. In other words, the Gospels asked, "How do you live?" rather than "What do you think?"

Matters of morality don't fall into the most important *de fide* category. They were developed by the magisterium—the church's teaching authority—not revealed in scripture or tradition.

Theologian Karl Rahner saw a discrepancy between the official teaching of the church and what the people really believe.[1] Most Catholics don't know a fraction of the official doctrine. But they must synthesize their faith with their life experience. To do so, "they must differentiate between more

[1] See "What the Church Officially Teaches and What the People Actually Believe," in *Theological Investigations,* vol. 22 (London: Darton, Longman and Todd, 1991), 165–75.

and less binding church teachings." Formed Christians must know what is central, and "while not denying, pay less attention to what is secondary."[2]

Careful reading of the Bible shows that it prohibits eating shrimp as well as killing people. How do we know that the latter takes priority? The doctrines of faith exist in the context of interpretation. For this reason, Catholics believe it's impossible to live by scripture only. The tradition of teaching also directs our quest.

Someone reading the *Catechism of the Catholic Church* might not know which teachings are most authoritative. All church teaching is presented there without instructions on how to interpret it. Here's a better image.

If it's helpful, visualize the church as a big house with many rooms. In the central courtyard are the crucial *de fide* doctrines. The word *doctrine* means "set a limit." Not believing in these would place one outside the walls of the house.

But surrounding that inner core are millions of rooms, all of which represent varying shades of belief. It's simply another way to look at the familiar line, "In my Father's house, there are many dwelling places" (Jn 14:2). How comforting to know it's roomy and welcoming in our eternal home.

SENSUS FIDELIUM

Another wonderful feature of Catholicism is the concept of *sensus fidelium* (the sense of the faithful). It means the people of God, inspired by the Spirit, together seek the best ways to put on the mind of Christ (see Phil 2:5; 2 Cor 10:5; 1 Cor 2:16). Therefore, any doctrine that is promulgated must also be received. If the collective wisdom of the people rejects it, it's useless to assert it.

The Immaculate Conception is an example of the *sensus fidelium* in action. Before its declaration as a doctrine of faith, most Catholics believed Mary was conceived without sin. The official decree was simply the magisterium of the church elevating a belief Catholics already held to the level of doctrine.

> The community of faith exists through the power of the Spirit. Thus, the Holy Spirit guarantees the church's mission: to proclaim the Gospel faithfully and to receive Christ. In scripture, this is most evident at Pentecost, when individuals were "all together" (Acts 2:1). Just as the Spirit inspired the first witness, so it keeps it alive today. "The Holy Spirit is the Church's living memory" (CCC 1099).

---

[2] Karl Rahner, "Reflections on the Adult Christian," *Theology Digest* 31 (1984): 125.

In the Eucharistic liturgy, the community acknowledges the Spirit as source of its unity through the epiclesis prayer, asking the Spirit to come upon the gifts. The presider prays over the bread and wine, which represent us, and asks the Spirit to transform them (and us) into Christ's body and blood.

Lumen Gentium 12 explains that the church's infallibility is rooted in the sensus fidelium of the whole People of God, manifest when that brings forth a consensus in matters of faith and morals. The treasure of faith is entrusted to the *whole* people—no privileged class nor insider information. As Jesus promised, the Advocate would anoint *all* disciples and lead them to truth (Jn 14:26).

The placement of Vatican II documents is significant. In *Lumen Gentium*, the chapter on the People of God comes before the chapter on the hierarchy. It's primarily through holy lives of people transformed by grace that the Gospel light shines forth. The church, then, is where God's gift of Jesus is received. The Spirit's presence is most obvious in the different cultures and contexts of local churches. Those varied forms of engagement with the gospel are displayed in painting, music, architecture, spirituality, and structures throughout time.

One theory about works of art, called "reception aesthetics," says they communicate on three levels—the producer, the work itself, the receiver. All three must be delicately balanced. The receiver is a co-producer because there is no effect without reception. For instance, if a novel is written but never read, nothing happens. So too for doctrine. If people accept a teaching and find meaningful application to their present context, it is accepted. If not, it's like a teacher or a singer talking or singing to themselves.[3]

Moral judgments aren't the exclusive responsibility of the hierarchy, but belong to the whole people of God. In fact, the laity's "wisdom and knowledge often arise from valuable life experience. Such wisdom is to be prized by church leaders" (*Constitution on the Church,* no. 38).

PRIMACY OF CONSCIENCE

This phrase seems to unleash a volley of argument, but the origins of the idea can be traced to early Christians' struggle with political government: "But Peter and the apostles answered, 'We must obey God rather than any

---

[3] Ormond Rush, *The Eyes of Faith: The Sense of the Faithful and the Church's Reception of Revelation* (Washington DC: Catholic University Press, 2009).

human authority'" (Acts 5:29). Later, Paul described the role of conscience, the universal sense of right and wrong, in reference to the Gentiles, who didn't know Jewish law. "They show that what the law requires is written on their hearts, to which their own conscience also bears witness" (Rom 2:15).

Later, theologian Thomas Aquinas wrote: "Conscience is more to be obeyed than authority imposed from the outside. By following a right conscience you not only do not incur sin but are also immune from sin, whatever superiors may say to the contrary" (*De veritate,* q. 17, a. 5). Furthermore, acting against conscience is a greater wrong than disobeying a superior. Conscience is more binding than external authority. Thomas also wrote: "Anyone who acts against his conscience always sins" (*Quaestiones quodlibetales,* 3, q. 12, a. 2).

St. John Henry Newman's "Letter to the Duke of Norfolk" contains a famous quotation about conscience: "If I am obliged to bring religion into after-dinner toasts . . . I shall drink—to the Pope, if you please—still, to Conscience first, and to the Pope afterward." Franz Jagerstatter, recently canonized, is an example of person who followed his conscience. The Nazis executed him in 1943 for treason because he would not cooperate with the regime.

The documents of Vatican II addressed conscience in several places. The *Declaration on Religious Freedom* states that we are bound to follow the truth as we know it. Even if the conscience is wrong, we have the obligation to follow it. Nor can anyone force us to act contrary to our conscience (no. 3). The *Constitution on the Church in the Modern World* affirms that "conscience is our most secret core and sanctuary. It is where we are alone with God, whose voice echoes in our depths" (no. 16).

Joseph Ratzinger, now Pope Benedict XVI, wrote in his *Commentary on the Documents of Vatican II*: "One's own conscience must be obeyed before all else, even if necessary against the requirement of ecclesiastical authority."

In *Forming Consciences for Faithful Citizenship*, the U.S. bishops acknowledge that "the responsibility to make choices in political life rests with each individual in the light of a properly formed conscience." That doesn't mean either of two extremes: blindly following church teaching *or* "anything goes." It *does* mean studying the question, knowing the teaching, and dialoguing respectfully with people we trust.

The question of primacy of conscience has surfaced during wars, and the church has supported the decisions of conscientious objectors to not engage in conflict. It also is intrinsic to questions of reproductive health and politics.

Michele Somerville, writing about the case of Father Roy Bourgeois for the October 20, 2011, issue of the *Huffington Post*, notes that primacy of conscience checks the mistakes of priests and even popes. It helps ensure that human failings "do not come between believers and their God. When it comes to God's truths the buck stops with the individual Catholic whom the Holy Spirit guides and enlightens."

INTERNAL FORUM

An example of this teaching made practical is the internal forum. A process of prayer and reflection, it sometimes leads to the decision that a marriage is no longer sacramental. In other words, it no longer symbolizes the union between Christ and his church. After discernment based on this understanding of matrimony, people sometimes believe they can remarry and receive the Eucharist. They arrive at the decision that the second marriage may be a blessing rather than a sin based on evidence that only they can know. It is the church's way of saying, "Here is the law. Interpret it with your common sense." It follows the lead of Jesus that we should live by the spirit, not the letter of the law.

Some theologians urge an end to the annulment system; in the meantime, they suggest that pastors make better use of the internal forum solution.

QUESTIONS FOR REFLECTION OR DISCUSSION

- Was anything in this chapter unfamiliar to you? If so, what? Do you agree or disagree with it?
- What are examples of the three "best-kept secrets" drawn from your own experience?
- What are the implications of these "secrets" in your life?

A Catholic Chorus

Adrienne: "I think of the Catholic Church as a massive family. Some are well-to-do, others not so much. But we're all welcome, and we know the same recipes (the sacraments and scriptures). Some relatives are whacky—you avoid them—and others you adore. Just like the church!"

Part II

The Seasons We Celebrate

Introduction

Feasts, Fasts, and Fun in the Catholic Calendar

If we think of faith as a mountain, then many paths lead to its summit. While some faith approaches emphasize the more doctrinal, logical aspects, others focus on action for justice, and still others on liturgy, ritual, and the arts. Different personality types respond best to different aspects, with some drawn to the intellectual, others to the active, and still others to the aesthetic. But regardless what particular path each person takes, the final goal is the same: achieve the mountaintop, union with God. From that peak, all can look back over their individual paths and admire their infinite variety.

This part develops in more detail the seasons in the Catholic year. We all know seasonal change from daily experience: the thunk of the Halloween pumpkin hitting the trash can; the first, anonymous bushes wearing a green haze in spring. In the church calendar, annual seasons also bring a feast or a fast, reasons for fun or the impetus to solitary prayer, which leads quite naturally into the first chapter in this part. As St. Hildegard of Bingen solemnly advised, "Be not lax in celebrating!"

Many writers have described the particularly Catholic genius of adapting to prevalent cultural customs. While this sometimes captures the worst of the culture, one of the best adaptations has been seasonal. For instance, the timing of Christmas coincides with the solstice feast when days started to grow longer around December 21. For Christians honoring the birth of Christ, the coming of more light worked on both literal and symbolic levels. Even in electrified modern settings, we still at some archetypal level fear winter's coming with its cold and darkness and rejoice in the light. In the words of the Celtic sea shanty,

We all join hands and form a chain
till the leaves of springtime come again!

Then there is Lent. We all need a time of "turning" from habitual ruts and Lent (meaning "springtime") provides it. Just as gardeners clear dead leaves and stalks to make way for new growth, so we assess our sorry selves and redirect our efforts.

The church also blessed the spring equinox, which more or less coincides with Easter. Something about the tenacity of green shoots poking through brown clay speaks of resurrection.

Much as we love the feasts that enliven each season, Richard Rohr adds a necessary caution: "If . . . people concentrate too much on special times, feasts, services, and seasons, they forget it is always now and here when God happens."[1]

That takes us back to sacramentality: the particularly Catholic belief that God pervades every time and season. There is no time or place where God cannot be found. The last two chapters in this part describe places dear to Catholics: parishes and retreat houses.

---

[1] *The Naked Now* (New York: Crossroad, 2009), 76.

Chapter 8

Catholic Identity

Narrow Box or Big Window?

What does it mean to be Catholic? There are probably as many answers to that question as there are Catholics. My own fascination with the identity question began, like most fascinations, in autobiography. I was educated by French nuns in a private girls' school. Academics were rigorous, and there wasn't much free time in the daily routine, except for one miraculous loophole that had escaped the sharp gaze of Reverend Mother: the chapel visit. During the last study hall of the day, we could visit the chapel. That meant waving a small square of black lace veil at the presiding sister, getting her nod, then escaping, unsupervised and independent, for the long walk down a hall filled with swooshing ferns and lined with huge windows. The gleaming wood floors made a fitting approach to the transcendent. There, a thoughtful person could transition from academic drudgery to sacred space.

Oddly enough, we didn't go simply to escape study. Perhaps brighter students had figured that out, but I went for the peace and beauty of that chapel. Half a century later I can still visualize its soaring white arches, its columns carved with intricate designs. Ivory marble predominated, anchored by glowing jewels of stained glass and polished surfaces of wooden pews. Getting A's in religion now seems less relevant to my future career than that lovely setting.

Those hushed and hidden moments in the chapel began a life-long love affair. I didn't know then that my personality type is intensely drawn toward beauty. I didn't realize how much an introvert needs a peaceful oasis in a day packed with interactions. Nor did I dream that my career in spirituality would one day lead back to the beginning.

But I began to connect the dots when I spoke to friends about similar, early experiences in Catholic schools. Artist Michael O'Neill McGrath, OSFS, dismayed by the academics of the classroom, delighted in the stained-glass windows of the church. Even as a first grader, he was itching for drawing paper and crayons, which foretold his stunningly creative career.

Father Paul Colloton, OP, director of education for National Pastoral Musicians, doesn't remember much about his classroom experience. But he glows with delight at the memories of choir. In that arena he came alive, foreshadowing his career as a liturgist and musician. All three of us had a *window*.

Our examples may not be true for everyone, but they suggest an interesting trend. In the question of Catholic identity, what some consider a side dish is indeed the main course. Many who have forgotten the precepts of the church or the essentials of transubstantiation remain faithful to the poetry of the faith: the smells and bells, the art and decoration, the saints and traditions.

Andrew Greeley, a sociologist who has studied fidelity to the church, writes: "Catholics stay in their Church because they like being Catholic, because of loyalty to the imagery of the Catholic imagination, because of pictures of a loving God present in creation, because of the spiritual vision of Catholics that they absorb in their childhood, along with and often despite all the rules and regulations that were drummed into their heads."[1] Which brings us to the question of narrow box or big window. Many people define Catholics in terms of what we oppose: abortion, same-sex marriage, the death penalty, to name a few current controversies. While those are important pieces, they don't create the whole picture. Nor is Catholicism simply cerebral. While study forms the strong spine of our theology, a larger dimension is accessible to those who may not be academically inclined. What, then, *are* we?

Being Catholic means being steeped in a way of life. It means finding God at every turn: in candlelight or conversation, in night sky or green meadow. No matter how small or even oppressive our environment may seem, we can look beyond or within it for a hidden dimension: the elusive, mysterious presence of God. All around us are signs, gifts from God. To read them aright, we need to interpret the language of symbol. Or, to stay with the metaphor, we need to open the windows for a larger perspective on human life—its divine element.

How do we best prepare children for this way of life, teaching its language, sensitizing them to its nuances?

As St. Ignatius directed, we go in through their door. Children are naturally attuned to the small miracles of creation: an intriguing insect, a puddle made for mirroring and splashing, an unusual cloudscape. They

---

[1] *The Catholic Myth* (New York: Simon and Schuster, 1990), 63.

are concrete minded, so abstractions have far less meaning than teachings grounded in sensate reality.

As the botanist Luther Burbank said: "Every child should have mud pies, grasshoppers, water-bugs, tadpoles, frogs and mud-turtles, elderberries, wild strawberries, acorns, chestnuts, trees to climb, brooks to wade in . . . bats, bees, butterflies . . . sand, snakes . . . and any child who has been deprived of these has been deprived of the best part of education." Lucky the child who knows the next level: that the grasshopper is a symbol of John the Baptist and the beehive represents the Christian community!

The best of Catholic worship accords with that.

As the book of Wisdom says, our delight in natural beauties guides us to their source, the author of all beauty. So the Advent fragrance of candles nestled in evergreen, the blaze of bonfire at the Easter Vigil, the splash of holy water, or the story of Jesus' post-resurrection barbecue beside the lake open the window through our senses to our eternal heritage.

Of course we must continue to teach the content of the faith: the gospel, social teachings, traditions. But let's also pay keen attention to the environment in which we teach that faith. Anyone who remembers the insufferable boredom of childhood—the endless days of *nothing to do*—knows the importance of feasts and fasts, snacks and treats, saints and stories, all open windows. Pope John XXIII evoked that image when he called the Second Vatican Council to let in some fresh air.

Are children in Catholic classrooms, whether parish schools or religious education programs, surrounded by symbol, color, art, statues that mirror *their* ethnicity, our finest music, our noblest saints, our most intriguing legends? Are we deliberate in our liturgies about using *real* candles, not the phony electric ones, *genuine* plants, not plastic greenery? Can we identify the turning of liturgical seasons by the choreography of colors? Have we forgotten the evocative play of incense and music?

Or have churches and classrooms become sterile boxes without windows to invite the play of imagination? In our efforts to educate business people and competent bureaucrats, are we neglecting the potential of budding artists and saints? Are we feeding peoples' spirits and senses as well as their consciences and minds?

We need to feed everyone, not just potential artists, poets, and musicians, with the same rich mix that fed the saints. In contrast, popular culture is thin gruel indeed. Christians have mountains to climb and a world to transform! They can't do that on a diet of pop tarts.

Catholics should be celebrating the saints' feasts, the liturgical seasons, multicultural customs, using decorations that aren't fluff but mirrors of God's image, icons into heaven. The root word for decoration in Latin is *decus*, which means "fitting." As Peter Mazar writes: "A real decoration makes the classroom a window into mystery."[2]

The early Christians, like ourselves, lived among many different cultures and belief systems. They had to compete, as we do, with other voices that appealed to their young. They couldn't hoard a treasure. They needed to display it openly for all to admire, with their finest language, loveliest hymns, and most beautiful art.

Nor were they threatened by the presence of other beliefs and value systems jostling for attention. St. Thomas Aquinas voiced this respect: "All that is true, by whomsoever it has been said, has its origin in the Spirit." The first disciples simply stood in their own truth, presenting it as well as they could, hospitably welcoming others to share. As our children grow up with multiculturalism, we'd be wise to model their stance.

QUESTIONS FOR REFLECTION OR DISCUSSION

- Does this chapter convince you that Catholicism isn't a narrow box but instead a big window? Why or why not?
- Give an example of a time you saw the divine in ordinary circumstances.

A Catholic Chorus

Annette: An art teacher who loves Catholicism for "all the great stuff, Annette probably refers to the statues, stained glass, holy water fountains and other paraphernalia found to varying degrees in Catholic churches. (One parish has gilded angels holding up the holy water font and candle holders, with millions of tiny lights illuminating multiple arches. If you remember the decorated front yard in the film "My Big Fat Greek Wedding," you get the picture.) Annette continues: "Some churches look bland as hotel conference rooms. I want to be the 'decorating bandit' and jazz them up!"

---

[2] *School Year, Church Year* (Chicago: Liturgy Training Publications, 2001), 26.

Chapter 9

Dealing with the Dark

The Feast of All Souls

It's impossible to praise the Catholic focus on light without giving equal weight to how we handle the darkness. In case the previous chapter left the impression of Pollyannas singing "Kumbaya" around the campfire in an endless summer, we must deal with inevitable darkness.

At the most natural, human level, "the sacred community" responds to those who mourn or face illness. It seems a small thing when facing a tremendous grief, but Catholics, like most believers, try to offer consolation in concrete ways. Illness, job loss, divorce, death: no one really knows what to say at such a time, which may be why the most eloquent consolations are wordless. A card, a touch, a casserole may not seem like much at the time. Grief can be all-absorbing, dulling the usual polite responses to small kindnesses. But later, people marvel that someone ill or elderly came to a funeral, that a friend offered a hug of comfort, or that another baked fresh bread.

It seems an especially Catholic trait to bring every human experience, including the darkness, to liturgy. It can carry us beyond even the great consolations human beings bring one another and into another realm. I never appreciated how this could happen until three people died in a year. Because I was close to them, a deep sadness was unresolved for a long time. My friend Kathy had battled inflammatory breast cancer for two years, fighting to stay alive for her husband and college-aged son and daughter. She died in January at the age of fifty-seven.

My son's friend Andy was an extreme skier, so active and vibrant, we feared he would die in a mountain climbing, biking, or kayaking accident. He walked into the hospital and died four hours later of strep pneumonia. He was thirty-two. His short time was packed with so many activities and loving relationships that it answered robustly the question of Mary Oliver, printed on the funeral program, "Tell me, what is it you plan to do with your one wild and precious life?"

My sister-in-law Beth, true to character, was sweet and uncomplaining about a prolonged, fierce backache. It was stage-four cancer. She died three weeks after her diagnosis at the age of fifty-six.

The stark facts don't reveal how we can be ambushed by grief, surprised by its spiral, especially when the three who died were young, their deaths unexpected. I wished my background were Mexican, so I could grieve openly in a community of other like-minded people during Los Dios de las Muertas (the days of the dead). Perhaps those customs, forged over centuries, could soothe aching hearts and unanswered questions. But they weren't my customs, inhaled like the fragrance of tortillas or roasting chilies in my youth. So the grief continued, as I hoarded memories of the dead and tried to stand with grieving relatives.

My friend Jeff, a Jesuit, once explained that concentric circles surround the deceased. In the first circle is the immediate family: spouse, parents, siblings, children. Behind them stand close friends and other relatives. Within the third circle stand those who knew the person but weren't intimate. It was important, Jeff suggested, to maintain our place within our circle, not stepping forward if we weren't closely connected in life. But by the same token, we couldn't step back: we needed to support those in the closer circles.

While I knew the importance of standing with the grieving, it still didn't resolve my own outrage that three marvelous people had died unfairly young and apparently healthy. None of the theological explanations made much sense.

Then I attended Mozart's *Requiem for All Souls' Day* at St. James Cathedral in Seattle. There I saw the power of ritual to carry our grief and unite us with loved ones at a level beyond language. The *Missa pro Defunctis* (mass for the dead) has been traditional since the fourteenth century, and its power continues today: surging, calming, uplifting, buoying up hope.

Any ritual guides us across a threshold into the unknown, and the passage from life to death is terrifying. Seeing others die who are like ourselves, we think of our own deaths. Are they imminent? Are we ready? The rite instills confidence, guiding and protecting us as it has many others making the same precarious crossing.

It was Catholic liturgy at its best: a solemn procession, candles and incense, awkward altar servers transformed into angelic icons, the Readings sung, all in a sweeping space that dwarfed the human beings. The golden vaults and massive crucifix proclaimed that we are not actors on a small stage here. We take our rightful, human place among saints, martyrs, cherubim and seraphim.

Our culture, dreading death, stuffs it away in a back drawer. Yet the "Dies Irae" trumpets it, calls it forth in politically incorrect terms, and unmasks it with a jolt. "Death will be stunned," the choir sings, and Paul echoes: "O death, where is your sting?" Limited and deluded creatures, we nevertheless have a great King whose majesty will annihilate threats to God's faithful ones. Almost timidly, the sung Sequence reminds God: "I am the reason for your journey; do not lose me on that day." On our final day nothing we've done for good or ill will matter much. The only thing that saves us is God's mercy.

The solemn Entrance Procession with many candles symbolizes a people journeying, coming from a secure source in God and moving deliberately toward a final destination, heaven. Our steps along the way may meander, but eventually we return to God who is our home. We move forward in the company of Sts. Peter and Paul, Catherine of Siena, Teresa of Avila, Joan of Arc, of Thomas More, Dorothy Day, the martyrs of El Salvador, of our grandparents, teachers, and friends, unseen but supportive companions.

Singing voices cascaded from the high arcs like a waterfall of compassion: "Et Lux perpetua luceat eis" (and let perpetual light shine upon them). For centuries we have asked two blessings on the dead: light and rest. That yearning might be attributed to medieval people working long hours in cold, dark conditions. But it still appeals. Light and rest sum up our dearest wish for our beloved, that they might abide, safe and happy within the gaze of Christ. John's Gospel doesn't use the word *pray*; instead, he repeats the verb *meno* (abide). With the best humans can muster in music, movement, and word, we lifted our loved ones into that state of grace.

Ultimately these rituals aren't so much for the deceased as for us who remain on earth, confused and angry. They assure us of another kingdom where death will be no more and every tear will be wiped away. We can't grapple with profound loss on the level of words. Much as I love words, and make my living from writing and speaking, I know how miserably words can fail. Before deep grief they sputter into silence or risk becoming pious platitudes, empty reassurance.

But music and ritual fill the space where words falter. They lift us into a place where, once again, we rejoin the beloved who have gone before us. We brush elbows in that communion of saints where time and space are no longer barriers separating us.

We turn instinctively to gestures such as the draping of the coffin with the funeral pall. It echoes the baptismal garment and is placed with special reverence by family members. Our pastor, inviting the children of an older woman to perform this symbolic act at her funeral, drew the parallel between parents tucking their children into bed at night and the adult children covering their mother for eternal sleep.

As the music swelled and filled every crevice of Seattle's cathedral, I remembered the smaller chapel where Kathy's funeral was held. It was a bitterly cold January day, and none of the pall bearers wore coats as we processed with our friend to the waiting hearse. It was a shock to leave the warm building and enter a light snowfall, but we were surprised and delighted to find women waiting, arms linked, all crying and freezing, creating a corridor of care.

We passed through them reverently, and when the mortuary assistant asked if we could lift the coffin, we answered ferociously, "Of course we can!" We had no idea whether we could carry that weight, but we couldn't abandon our friend to strangers. As her husband pointed out later, "You've been carrying Kathy for the last two years."

We'll try to continue her work in inner-city schools. We've begun a scholarship in her name and will tutor and read to children as she did. It seems true to the message of Jesus, who encouraged us to continue his work.

Andy's friends began a fund for others to become certified as elementary-school principals, a degree he completed just before he died.

Beth's children brought books and toys to the kids attending her funeral, just as she would have done.

What is important lives on.

The scripture read at the Mass for the Dead was John 14:1–6, in which Jesus reassures his disciples that in his Father's house, there are many dwelling places. It made me wonder about hidden rooms: Did Kathy wait at the end of a hallway, Andy in an adjoining garden, or Beth on another porch? Were we like people staring at the sun, unable to see them because their light was too dazzling?

Karl Rahner suggests that our biggest mistake is imagining that the dead have left us. Instead, he says, they remain with us, invisible and inaudible, but even larger than in life. The Irish writer John O'Donohue, who also died young, wrote, "Perhaps one of the surprises of death will be a retrospective view of the lives we lived here and to see how our friends among the dead clothed us in weave after weave of blessing"—and what a warm and heathery tweed that must be.[1]

Of all the writers to grapple with the problem of death, Paul identified it most clearly not as an end but as a swift shift: "We will all be changed, in a moment, in the twinkling of an eye, at the last trumpet" (1 Cor 15:51–52). O'Donohue adds that when we have worked through our grief we will

1 *To Bless the Space Between Us* (New York: Doubleday, 2008), 212.

Be able to enter the hearth
In your soul where your loved one
Has awaited your return
All the time.[2]

The beauty of music, the vastness of the church, and the reassurance of light and rest bring a foretaste of that reunion. Then we will laugh with our loved ones again, feel their touch on shoulder or hand, share a meal, and rejoice in the goodness of a God who has brought us together, this time forever.

QUESTIONS FOR REFLECTION OR DISCUSSION

- When words fail, what can take their place?
- Has ritual ever helped you through the grieving process? If so, how?

A Catholic Chorus

Maureen: "Nobody does a funeral as well as the Catholics! Or the Holy Week services!"

The church gives a place where we can turn in tragedy. Older people remember that in Catholic schools, the news of President Kennedy's death was met with an immediate trip to church or chapel. At that time there was general admiration for the fact that whether you were a janitor or the president of the United States, the ritual was the same.

That's also been true for subsequent disasters such as 9/11 or the school shooting at Columbine. Faith gives us a place to stand while we search for answers. And if there are answers to such tragedy, perhaps they can be found in following a God who suffered and died. At times of profound grief, the ritual prayed since the ninth century offers the best encouragement we have: "May the angels lead you into paradise; may the martyrs come to welcome you and take you to the holy city, the new and eternal Jerusalem" (Order of Christian Funerals).

Sister Genevieve Glen, OSB, comments on the reasoning behind the ritual. We accompany our dead until we start relinquishing them to those who lead them

---

[2] Ibid., 118.

beyond this world. She writes: "We accompany our dead because we love them. We accompany our dead because we believe they live."[3]

[3] "In paradisum," *Give Us This Day*, a periodical published by Liturgical Press, Collegeville, MN (November 2011), 9.

Chapter 10

Advent

A Season of Surprise

During an Advent session at Mater Dolorosa Parish in San Francisco, one lady stoutly maintained she *hated* surprises. During a raffle afterward, *she* won the turkey!

Such unexpected events help prepare us for Advent, the season of a surprising spirituality. God, who could have become human as a respected philosopher like Plato, a military leader like Alexander the Great, or a beautiful queen like Cleopatra, comes instead as a helpless baby. All the Beauty and Power in the universe becomes vulnerable and dependent. Furthermore, God pitches a tent, not only "among" us, but "*in*" us, as some translations say. What an odd residence for the King of kings!

As *Gaudium et spes* says: God "has in a certain way united himself with each individual. He worked with human hands, he thought with a human mind. He acted with a human will and with a human heart he loved" (no. 22). Advent is meant as a time of preparation for that incarnation event, but how can we prepare for something so impossible to imagine?

One answer lies in the direct interplay between scripture and our lived experience. It seems as if God always makes an entrance through the door *behind* us, the place where we *weren't* looking. That pattern, also found in the Bible, sensitizes us to look beyond the tried-and-true, socially sanctioned, boring, repetitious rut. As some say, God lurks in the cracks between certainties.

Promise came to the Samaritan woman in a surprising way (Jn 4:7–42). She trudged to the well as she had nine million other times, but there she met a stranger who snagged her attention. His request was preposterous. This guy without a bucket wasn't supposed to use the vessel of a less orthodox Jew! Nor was he supposed to talk with a woman in public. He didn't make a demand but suggested a possibility: If only you knew the gift of God . . .

It's the kind of tantalizing potential children suspect before Christmas. If only you knew what was in that large box with the intriguing tag. How could the woman at the well resist such a mysterious invitation?

Until then, she'd probably done what she had to do to survive: endless drudgery, reliance on men since she had few rights, enduring the sneers of self-righteous, married-only-once women. The stranger offers her another way, an inner source of vitality that will never dry up or disappoint. He presents God's life in terms she understands. Who appreciates a fountain more than a desert dweller? She can practically taste fresh drops on her tongue.

Jesus himself isn't immune to the effects of a long, hot walk. Angels don't rush in with iced pitchers and shading umbrellas. Like us, he depends on human beings to relieve his human needs. In the architecture of John's Gospel, the request recurs during the crucifixion: "I thirst" (19:28). Furthermore, he doesn't use flowery camouflage, but speaks the need, simply and directly. As St. Augustine pointed out, Jesus' weariness may spring symbolically from his long journey into humankind, with its flaws and evils.

We all function in familiar grooves; it's how we organize our time. Especially during this super-busy season, various chores compete for our attention, screaming, "Attend to me!" "No, me!" "I'm next!" Like a chorus of toddlers, all these jobs demand time and energy. It's tempting to strangle those who want us to be still and quiet in Advent prayerfulness.

And yet . . . Scripture scholar Thomas Brodie says the woman at the well was too preoccupied with daily necessities. She had to learn to relax and enjoy God.[1] For people obsessed with responsibility, as many are before Christmas, it's wondrous relief to let God be God. And one of God's hallmarks seems to be this propensity to surprise.

In the Last Judgment scene, both the "sheep" and the "goats" are surprised by the king's words (Mt 25:31–46). Apparently what they thought important wasn't and vice versa. "You mean that pbj sandwich I made for my daughter? That tea I gave the repair man? *That*'s where you were? Not in attending church, the solemn committee meetings, the dutiful donations?"

What may block our awareness is the same pressure that swamped the Samaritan woman. Picture them jostling, all contenders for our attention, but ultimately impostors. Someone must muscle them aside if the King is to claim the throne, centrality in our lives. Then, as the Buddhists say, if we think we've achieved *that*, we probably aren't there yet. Surprise!

One reaction to Jesus mentioned fairly often in the Gospels is astonishment. He so often breaks the mold of *How the Messiah Ought to Be.* He certainly disrupted Mary's routine—even before he was born. Even now

---

1 *The Gospel according to John* (New York: Oxford University Press, 1993).

in the Middle East, women pregnant before marriage are stoned to death. She faced that possibility—and certain shame. All surprises aren't pleasant. Some have the potential for disaster.

But the angel reassures Mary, whose natural response is shock. As Fran Ferder writes, "A life of fear is not what God has in mind for Mary, or for any of us. . . . Mary and God change her tragedy into a love story of epic proportions. But not right away."[2] The last phrase is significant. The vision Isaiah holds up throughout Advent is one of dead stumps flowering, harmony among enemies. If we look at the world scene today, we see how such change comes in slow increments. And yet, as Habakkuk reminds us, "The vision . . . will surely come" (2:2–3).

We are treated to brief glimpses of the lion and lamb resting together: Fr. Greg Boyle, SJ, brings warring gang members to cooperate in his Los Angeles Homeboy Industries. Those who once fired bullets at each other now fire text messages. Such dramatic change can happen on a large scale, or when estranged family members reconcile, or when we welcome less comfortable parts of ourselves. The lion doesn't sprout fur or the lamb roar; each animal remains itself, distinct, yet not drowning out the other.

Commenting on the "peaceable kingdom" theme of Advent, a woman who'd watched the pecking order of lions at their watering hole in Africa observed: "The larger ones definitely go first. But once the lion is satisfied, he won't attack randomly." St. Francis of Assisi knew this too. When the citizens of Gubbio were terrified of a marauding wolf, he advised: "Feed the wolf." So too for our inner hungers. If they are satisfied, we can begin the long, slow process of disarming the heart.

Our Advent yearning is not for Christ to come; he already has come in history. We long for our world to be saturated with the gospel, permeated with Christ's presence, and our hearts to become more compassionate. His unpredictability then directs us to embrace events that may disrupt our routines.

If we dread the season that alerts us to *All We Haven't Done for Christmas,* we're missing wonder unfolding before our eyes. The four weeks scroll through the magnificent history of human hope, and we concentrate on catalogues. Or we clip recipes, watch the sales, and agonize over what to get Aunt Lucy. Advent asks us to take a deliberate stand that says: "Over centuries, people yearned for Christ's coming, so I won't take it for granted. I'll never let his incarnation be rubbed away by busyness."

Some surprises should astound us: Peoples' kind efforts to help us, even when they are busy or tired themselves; the discovery of many options in a situation that seemed a dead end; a sympathetic friend in a wildly

---

[2] *Enter the Story* (Maryknoll, NY: Orbis Books, 2010), 28, 31.

dysfunctional office; a window of time in a packed schedule; a flash of beauty; a check in the mail; a stimulating conversation in an otherwise empty day; someone's contribution of last night's leftovers the day we forgot to bring lunch to work. Hunting for the surprises tucked into each day eventually builds a perennial hope, a stubborn refusal to believe that God brings us anything but ultimate joy. If we know that the story ends happily, why waste time on worry?

Poet Mary Oliver in "The Kingfisher" qualifies that small surprises don't mean unmitigated bliss, but make fine stepping stones through the ordinary:

—so long as you don't mind
a little dying, how could there be a day in your whole life
that doesn't have its splash of happiness?

What if Advent isn't an exhausting list of duties but a marvelous scavenger hunt where we keep discovering tantalizing clues of a *good* master? What if God shares our delicious delight and high expectation in planning a surprise for a dear friend or child? What if God's coming is like that of someone deeply loved, for whom it is sheer joy to bake, clean, shop, and decorate? What if all the preparation time vanishes as nothing to the enormous relief of seeing and holding that loved one? "What ifs?" attune us to surprising promises—what Advent is all about.

QUESTIONS FOR REFLECTION OR DISCUSSION

- What is your initial response to the word *surprise*?
- Do you find surprises positive? negative? both?
- Why do you think God sends so many surprises?
- If you'd previously thought of Advent as somewhat grim and forbidding, does this chapter change your attitude in any way?

A Catholic Chorus

Deidre: A children's author and speaker, a native of Scotland, Deirdre's brogue bubbles through her response: "Ignatian spirituality—I love being a follower of Ignatius and spending this life trying to find God in all things! Mind you, I do also love St. Patrick and how he managed to bring Christianity to Ireland while still honoring the Celtic love for the fairies. And . . . I love the feast of All Saints. Oh, and Thomas Merton . . . and Anthony de Mello."

Her husband chimes in, "Being able to go to mass on Saturday evening!" And her daughter adds, "I'm very grateful for Catholic education—from the little convent I went to in England, to a high school run by the Sisters of Loretto, to Georgetown in Washington DC."

Chapter 11

Christmas Themes

Every time it happens, I catch my breath. Westbound flights to California pass over the Grand Canyon in silence. Beneath us stretches a marvelous sculpture of brilliant red rock, carved over centuries by the Colorado River. J. B. Priestley called it "all Beethoven's nine symphonies in stone and magic light."

Seven million years of geological history lie exposed beneath the plane, and the pilot very seldom mentions it. Passengers on Flight 1183 to San Diego or 1719 to Santa Ana doze, read magazines, or work on their laptops. "Hey!" I'd shout if security wouldn't arrest me. "There are only seven natural wonders of the world, and you're missing one of them!"

Are we equally oblivious to Christmas when it rolls around again? Some things are so important that, once a year, we must make a conscious effort to remember them. The themes of attention, trust and celebration are so frail they tend to get swamped in seasonal busyness. But they are so powerful they can sustain us through the rest of the year.

A certain "amnesia" is healthy for humans: the mind simply can't hold all the details, phone numbers, passwords, jingles, events, and so on that threaten to clog and stall it. It's as natural to erase the mental clutter as to clean out the garage.

But the hazard of this natural forgetfulness is that it works against our remembering how we've negotiated difficult passages before—illness, job loss, divorce, grief, moving—so we can do it again. Christmas, like the weekly Eucharist, recalls our survival stories.

ATTENTION

During Advent, the themes, like those of music, begin to build gently, then reach a climax in Christmas. First comes our transition from ordinary time. Isaiah sounds the alert: "A voice cries out: In the wilderness, prepare the way of the Lord" (40:3). Notice the placement of the colon. The good news comes first to the desert where it's most needed. There, all is bleak and empty, unless you've got a *long* extension cord and a *lot* of water. It's a wasteland without borders where nothing works the way it does in cozy civilization.

We're always in one wilderness or another. One year it is drought, dismal economy, and widespread joblessness. Another year it might be poor health or the death of a friend. Yet the advice remains the same: always look for the water sources. One year we're sustained by kind people; another, by the hope of recovery.

Furthermore, Isaiah continues, "Make straight in the desert a highway for our God" (40:3). The purpose of a highway is to keep moving, not to get snagged or stuck in the desert. The prophet recalls our high calling as God's construction crew, with lots of work to do. We are *not* to get sucked into anxiety or worry about what we can't control anyway. The desert plays its part in awakening us, but we don't want to stall there.

Where are we getting bogged down, building roadblocks to God? For some people it is depression or a hurt they can't release; for others, a debilitating illness. Even innocent victims of crime can feel responsible, and guilt or shame drains energy. When we're trapped in terrible circumstances, we can remember the Jews in the Nazi camps. Some went to the ovens angry and bitter; others went singing the psalms. When the problem is unavoidable, which response do we choose?

Each year Christmas reminds us that we needn't get trapped by whatever it is that threatens to sap our strength. We are beloved of God, centers of freedom and fidelity.

Throughout the Genesis account of creation, one refrain sounds over and over: "and God saw that it was good." The word *good* refers to the stars and sea, the land and plants, the rivers and animals. But as the account reaches its crescendo, the creation of human beings, it shifts to the Hebrew word *tov.* This means blessed, growing toward completeness. While flowers and fish have reached their natural perfection—they can't get any better by making retreats or taking classes—humans are still in process. We always have the potential to grow into what God envisioned at our conception.

TRUST

As we make our wobbly way toward God's dream for us, the only door to the future is trust. Trusting is not an act like leaping off a cliff, but faith solidly rooted in past experience. As Pat Livingston says, "It's impossible to trust God in the abstract or just because we're told God is trustworthy.

. . . We learn to trust God because of our ongoing experiences of God's goodness."[1]

We've all had blessings slide into our foundering boats like full nets of fish, thrashing and gleaming in the sun. This is the time to remember that God, who has been faithful before, will be faithful again. No matter what desert or wasteland we face, God enters it with us because of Jesus' incarnation.

Much troubles us, but much has already been resolved. Look, for instance, at an old "to do" list. It records chores crossed off, projects accomplished, calls returned, questions answered, and dilemmas either solved or forgotten. All the prickly question marks eventually bend into a smooth highway for God.

Researchers who study happiness find a close correlation between happiness and trust. If we can engage confidently with our government, church, workplace, school, or neighbors, we feel supported, and in turn, able to trust.

CELEBRATION

John's first letter says God's commands "are not burdensome for whoever is born of God conquers the world" (1 Jn 5:3–4). Our learning to trust may be the work of great happiness that leads to Christmas. Then we celebrate the fact that God "pitched his tent *in* us" (Jn 1:14).

What's waiting to be birthed in us? If we dismiss that possibility because we're too old, tired, sick, or angry, it's the season to remember Elizabeth. She and her husband assumed they were too old to have a child, but John the Baptist was God's surprise.

Another surprise was God's choice of the most unlikely vehicle, the person who seemed least suited to bring his son into the world. Mary had four strikes against her: she was female, young, unmarried, and a Jew, belonging to the ethnic group oppressed by Romans, clearly the dominant culture with all the power. But apparently God didn't think human obstacles and categories were "flaws" in Mary. If God had approached a heavenly committee to explain the "Plan for Salvation," God would have been unfazed by the ensuing chorus of criticism.

Scripture doesn't record whether a goose was present at the Bethlehem stable. But symbolically, it would be appropriate. Nicholas Kristof recalls that his family raised geese when he was a boy in Oregon. The geese mate

---

[1] *Let in the Light* (Notre Dame, IN: Ave Maria Press, 2006), 108.

for life, and trying to fatten up the male with some delicacy, like a dish of corn, was impossible; "they would take it all home to their true loves."

The boy's monthly job was to grab a goose for slaughter. As it struggled in his arms, another goose "would bravely step away from the panicked flock and walk tremulously toward me. It would be the mate of the one I had caught, male or female, and it would step right up to me, protesting pitifully. It would be frightened out of its wits, but still determined to stand with and comfort its lover."[2] The adult Jesus would do that: step forward to stand with us, sacrificing his very life. At our best, we do that for others—fearful, unsure, yet stepping forward for those we love. At this season we gratefully celebrate holy boldness.

When we reach Christmas itself, our pastor, Father Patrick Dolan, recommends in his homily, "For one day, let the child in the manger overshadow the elephant in the living room." Of course we have issues when we gather with our families to celebrate the feast. Old arguments can resurface nastily; old wounds can reemerge; old habits can still grate. But all we need do to better appreciate our friends and relatives is notice how many have died, how many mourn. Despite his annoying repetitions, we're blessed to still have Grandpa. Despite their astronomical costs, we'll miss our children when they grow up and move away.

The Christ Child reminds us that even the small, vulnerable, and insecure can make a giant contribution. As an infant he demonstrated silently what he would say strongly as an adult: the prince of this world has no hold over me. The brute force of the Roman Empire, Herod's murderous thugs: *Nothing* could stop a baby and his bewildered parents from bringing forgiveness. When God asks us to be God's hearts, hands, and home in our worlds, do we respond hesitantly or fearfully?

If so, we need the central word: *Remember.* The forces that drag us down and demoralize us have no power because we belong to God. Even as we struggle to believe and internalize that wondrously good news, it's giving us life. Christmas reminds us how we were saved once—and will be saved again and again and again. Jesus wants to come into our lives, take on human skin and elbows and ears, heal whatever it is that holds us back from being fully ourselves, fully God's. Like bells on a frosty morning, the themes resound: Attend. Trust. Celebrate.

QUESTIONS FOR REFLECTION OR DISCUSSION

- Choose one idea in this chapter for further reflection. What emerges?
- Does anything here shift your thinking about Christmas?

---

[2] Nicholas Kristof, "A Farm Boy Reflects," *The New York Times* (July 31, 2008).

A Catholic Chorus

Claire: Now an editor for a Catholic publisher, Claire converted as a young adult and writes of her love for the church: "Catholicism gives me the most appropriate tools for experiencing and responding to the divine and for working out my mission on earth. I am a 'material girl,' particularly sensitive to the visual, as well as the other senses. The sacramentality of Catholicism allows me to make the connection to the sacred through the channels that flow the best for me. I am fascinated by the ways that humans interpret the spiritual through the material and the countless ways that we arrange the material world in order to create spiritual paths for each other. I love being in community, worshiping in community, and serving together in community. I love the sense of a tradition that runs through history and yet is constantly reshaped (though often contentiously!) for each generation. Of course there are plenty of problems with this human institution; I am plenty critical. But the core is life giving. I need it and I think it needs me."

Later, Claire speaks of her background: "The Christian Science church where I grew up was stark and plain. I'm grateful to them for many truths—and a religion founded by a woman (Mary Baker Eddy)! But they weren't into sacramentality—they believe the things you see around you are error, don't exist. In a sense, you weren't to enjoy too much or get too enthralled with the things of earth. The subtext was, Satan can grab and affect you. Evil can lead you into unhelpful paths. Don't believe in a water baptism—it's a spiritual affair. I felt an emptiness, since the spiritual realm had to be completely imagined—I couldn't see or hear any of it. From Catholics, I heard the opposite, that the things of earth are good, a window to the spiritual.

"My mother was trying to be a good Christian Scientist for the sake of her relationship with her mother-in-law and husband. But Mom felt she'd failed. After my cold became pneumonia, she went to a doctor, which that religion doesn't condone!

"All the early signs told me about holy objects creating a sacred space. When I went with the Episcopal family across the street to a Christmas Eve service, it was manna! I loved the bells, the kneeling, the incense, the creche, the music! Something about those objects made me feel holiness, and I wanted to bask in it. Afterward, I genuflected to everything.

"Another childhood friend was Catholic. Her oldest brother wanted to be a priest. I was attracted to her family. We also attended a Jewish friend's brother's

bar mitzvah, so I appreciated different traditions, but Catholic and Jewish looked like more fun.

"As a Methodist in California, I sang in choir at a lovely church. It had a cross with water streaming down it. Before we moved to Florida, I prayed to it: "I have to go away. Please be with me!"

"My family was moral and prayed, but had no sense of hush or mystery—it was all matter of fact. They didn't want to think much about the crucifixion, saying, 'We don't dwell on those things.' There was too much emphasis on sin and evil.

"As a graduate student at Indiana University, my roommate was Catholic. She wanted to go to daily mass but couldn't go alone—so I went with her. Then I joined a Hindu cult for a while—very interesting. I loved meditation; it helped me see Jesus as a spiritual master, a guru. I could look at him again without the Sunday School eyes.

"Working on my doctorate at the University of Chicago, I passed a Catholic church with Spanish architecture every day. I was studying medieval art and getting more intrigued. I remember standing outside the convent, thinking 'there's gotta be a way to get in there!' My sponsor in Overeaters Anonymous said Catholicism was part of her twelve-step program. Finally in church (it helped that it was liberal), the lady beside me held my hand for the Our Father and said, 'Oh, dear, your hand is so cold!' Afterward, the priest welcomed me: 'Hi, I'm Jack.' I assumed he knew I wasn't Catholic, but it turned out the parish was just friendly; after masses, five priests stood outside, welcoming.

"In the community were scripture scholars who knew Latin and Greek, and taught at the University of Chicago. Gradually I realized mass was the happiest hour of the week–I was smitten. So, through RCIA, I fell head over heels in love with liturgy. But at the last minute, I got cold feet. I didn't like pro-lifers and how they behaved. My family had been pro-choice, not pro-abortion. A priest said, 'Look at essentials, the Creed. Are you willing to be open to other things? Then come on in!'

"Coming into the church was the most dramatic thing that ever happened to me. It was like entering a loving family, so different from competitive graduate school. I wanted to immerse myself as completely as I could.

"At times now, difficulties with the church rise up and the original glow fades slightly. But the liturgy brings it back. When it's done well, it's remarkable. That's how I want to spend my life—making it for other people what it's been

for me. My husband has both deep wisdom and deep anger, so he's a good partner to work through what we both love and dislike about the church. I guess it comes down to that unanswered question, 'Lord, where should we go?' I can find good people other places, but not this liturgy. I'd be hungry.

"When I meet cradle Catholics, especially articulate ones, I drink in their stories—just fascinating! My 'inculturation into the tribe' continues, since I still have weird missing pieces. For instance, I don't know the Act of Contrition!"

Chapter 12

Lent

Places to Pause

An annual season of penance and reflection is common to many traditions, for example, the Islamic Ramadan. So what makes a Catholic Lent unique? What are its best parts?

As with most things Catholic, a big part of the answer lies in the sensory connections. Sometimes, in giving a catechetical workshop, I've asked the audience members to remember the Lents of their childhoods. A wealth of sense impressions emerges: the fragrance of incense, the singing of "Stabat Mater," the taste of tuna casserole or fish sticks on Friday, the soft swish of ashes on a forehead, and with older people, the draping of the statues in purple. No one ever mentions the headier doctrines. Instead, it's immediately clear: messages engraved on all five senses endure. So while the following is not a complete or doctrinal approach to Lent, it describes some of the highlights that have touched people enough to change their lives.

LENT BEGINS: ASH WEDNESDAY

People unaware of this day may wonder why coworkers or passers-by have a large smudge of what looks like dirt on their foreheads. This is part of a ritual where ashes are marked in the form of a cross on each participant. A slight change in the formula spoken when ashes are given is significant: "Turn from sin and trust the good news." Sin in the Hebrew context is anything less than the fullness of what God wants us to become. While the media and the grapevine may hum with news of "giving up" (alcohol, chocolate, meat, and so on) for Lent, the real fast is from what destroys us—the bad memories, overstimulation, and worries that will sicken us if we focus on them.

No matter what the darkness in our past (argument, illness, divorce, betrayal), the dynamic of Lent is to name it, not deny it, treat loss with gentle kindness, then move on. Whatever vortex threatens to suck us in, we look to the hope offered by Jesus, his dear and welcoming embrace. We know we can make this passage because we've done it before, just as our spiritual ancestors, the Jews, left the slavery of Egypt.

SETTING THE TONE

Whatever Jesus goes through, he breathes into us. The story told on the first Sunday of Lent, about Jesus' temptation, sets the tone for the season to follow. So, if Jesus endures a desert struggle, so do we. If he must assess his priorities in response to the devil's challenges, so must we. And if he turns from the dark, destructive voice to the life-giving one, we do the same.

It's an excellent time to ask ourselves, as we should regularly, *What's going on inside? What am I hungering for? What matters most?* Lent is the ideal time to tackle the tough questions: *Where have we become inauthentic or sluggish? What have we neglected? Where do we need to spend more time, money or energy? How have we squandered our gifts?* Knowing that physical privations are secondary to emotional suffering, we burrow deep into the soul. *What obstacles block the pathway to God? What selfishness strains our compassion for others?*

Jesus' integrity and earnestness are born of his desert experience. In that harsh environment he could have died. Because he survived, he can speak authentically of God's sustaining presence there—or anywhere. Just as Jesus would say that the prince of this world had no hold on him, so we too belong to God, not to anything that threatens us.

Prayer, fasting, and almsgiving are traditional Lenten practices. The first is a call to live more reflectively, taking time with God, reading scripture or other inspirational books, journaling, listening for God's voice in the silence. The second isn't guilty dieting but a practice found in many religious traditions that encourages us to say no to ourselves, focusing instead on our hunger for God. In solidarity with the hungry throughout the world, we create an empty space for God to fill. Fasting reminds us that humans don't live by bread alone and that restricting our physical pleasures can turn us toward spiritual richness. Almsgiving, what we do for others, springs from gratitude that God has given us much. If money is tight, we clean out closets, donating clothes that don't fit or household objects that aren't used.

HOLY THURSDAY

Jesus' words at the Last Supper are important because they occur so near the end of his life, a privileged time. Here Jesus addresses one of the hardest things in any relationship—saying a final goodbye. To help retreatants appreciate this gospel section (Jn 14–17), I've asked them, "If you knew you were going to die tomorrow, what would you want to tell your loved ones?" Given the narrow time frame, they focus on what's really important and forget petty concerns. Like the goodbye calls on 9/11, the content is nothing but love.

Likewise, Jesus' final discourse contains precious gold. Rarely does he mention sin. (So too, if we were telling our children, spouse, relatives, or friends goodbye, it's doubtful that we would catalogue their failures.) Instead, he speaks of a flow of love that began in creation and that must wash even protesting Peter. "Unless I wash you, you will have no inheritance with me" (Jn 13:8). The stream image continues in the words of the mass when the presider addresses God as "the fountain of all holiness."

JESUS BETRAYED

What we may need most in grief is presence. A woman dealing with multiple losses said appreciatively of her counselor, "I told her this was a 4–Kleenex day!"

That is our first, feeling response. Those who share it with us perform an important work of mercy. But at another level, human beings strive for understanding. Our urge to make meaning underlies the natural question, why? When we face distress, we seek other people of faith standing in a tradition to help us ground our sorrow within the meaning of Christ's suffering.

That was exactly the frame of reference used by a woman visiting her brother Frank in the burn unit of a hospital. A nurse asked if she'd seen Mel Gibson's film, "The Passion." "Why would I need to see that?" she replied. "If I wanted to see the passion, all I'd need to do is watch you change Frank's dressings."

Healthy people reject a God who would cause pain. But they are drawn to one who suffers with them.

In Luke's account (22:48) of the betrayal, Jesus seems startled when Judas approaches him in the garden. "Judas, do you betray the Son of Man with a kiss?" he asks. The symbol of love twisted to betrayal mirrors the deepest human sorrow. We are hurt the most by those we love; the others we don't care that much about.

Yet even before Judas's lips have lifted from Jesus' cheek, before the kiss has dried, comes forgiveness. Within Jesus is a deep pool of compassion, also experienced by the woman taken in adultery, the paralytic lowered through the roof, and the man born blind. How hard it must be for Judas to expect revulsion and find instead unrelenting love. How hard it is for us, expecting retribution, to discover instead the infinite well of mercy.

As if Judas's betrayal weren't enough, Jesus must endure Peter's too. After Peter's triple denial, one line is heartbreaking: "The Lord turned around and looked straight at Peter" (22:61). What hurt that look must contain; it prompts Peter to "weep bitterly."

But another emotion is there as well, a hope that prompts Peter to repent. He and Judas do the same thing, but respond differently. When Jesus asks, "Do you love me?" three times, and Peter answers yes, the slate is wiped clean. He is completely forgiven.

The message this Gospel contains is that there is nothing Jesus cannot forgive. We live out the rest of our lives within that look, knowing that it falls not only on us but on our most despised enemy. No matter what any of us have done, we simply cannot move outside the circle of God's compassion.

GOOD FRIDAY LITURGY

Many wise traditions know the importance of naming one's loss or sorrow, since suppressing it only makes it worse. Indeed, Thich Nhat Hanh suggests cradling our broken hearts as tenderly as we would a sick and crying child. In a particularly Catholic way, abstraction such as suffering is translated to tangible, visible word and gesture in the liturgy. Furthermore, it links our individual stories and struggles concretely, not just verbally, to the over-arching story of Christ's redemptive suffering.

My rule of thumb for Good Friday liturgy is "when we do something only once a year, pay attention." So I focus on three parts of the service that move me especially.

The Presider's Prostration: Catholic liturgy at its best speaks through symbol or gesture, not needing many words to convey meaning. For instance, submersion in the waters of baptism, lighting the Easter candle, or offering a cup of wine all speak eloquently without words.

The Good Friday service begins with a silent procession (robust singing would be completely out of place), and the presider prostrating himself before the altar. We see this action only once a year. What does it say? Different people probably have different interpretations at different times of their lives. To me, it says starkly, "We killed God." Not to become morbid, but to some extent, we are all guilty. We have killed that divine spark in one another through a callous word, a harsh condemnation, a heavy hand.

The presider speaks for all of us as he lies face down on the floor. "This, my friends, is what we've done to the finest human/divine being who ever lived." Words can't touch the tragedy: symbolically, we all lie flat on our faces.

The Readings (Psalm 22): The first verbal nugget is the taunting line from the reading: "He relied on the Lord; let him deliver him,/ let him rescue him, if he loves him" (Ps 22:9). *If* God loves him?

Jesus, who began praying this psalm from the cross, must have suffered the ultimate abandonment: doubt that his Father, who had always been his source of joy and strength, loved him. Fully human, not just play-acting, he descended to the depths of human exile. Yet, the psalms have a remarkable way of pirouetting from one emotion to another, often from depth to peak.

Scripture scholar Kathy McGovern presents a positive interpretation on "The Story and You" website:

> In his agony, Jesus the Jew calls out the beginning verse of that well-known psalm of lament: "My God, my God, why have you abandoned me?" There are some women "standing at a distance" who have followed him since he set out from Galilee to Jerusalem. They surely know this psalm, and in synagogue style they respond to his introduction by reciting the rest of it, all 31 verses, including the triumphant end, when the suffering one proclaims that "all will proclaim the Lord to generations still to come, his righteousness to a people yet unborn. . . ."
>
> Jesus . . . calls out the first verse of Psalm 22 with his last breaths, knowing that "those standing at a distance"—and that's us, too, isn't it?—will respond by praying the rest of the psalm for him.

In the context of the crucifixion the psalm offers a tribute to prayer under the worst conditions: "You who fear the Lord, praise him." At some unspoken depth, Jesus knows that ultimately it all ends well, as God had planned.

The Passion: The reading from the passion according to John follows Jesus from his questioning by Annas the high priest to the praetorium where he is tried by Pilate. The time frame for most of chapter 18 occurs at night. After the last supper, Jesus goes to the garden in darkness. Judas comes with soldiers bearing lanterns and torches. They bring him to the court of Annas. There Peter's denials occur by the charcoal fire; it is still night. But chapter 18:28 records that "it was morning." That raises the question, where did Jesus spend the night?

McGovern gives a fascinating talk about Holy Week, with slides taken in the Holy Land. One of her most vivid descriptions is of a dark, spidery, terrifying pit. Prisoners who'd been taken into custody were lowered into it by pulleys and kept chained there so they wouldn't kill themselves before their trial. It is most likely, she concludes, that Jesus would have spent the night before his trial by Pilate in this dank dungeon.

The Light of the World plunged into terrible darkness and chained there. What were Jesus' thoughts? Clearly, he wouldn't have been able to sleep much. Did he pray? Did he console other prisoners? Did he remember his friends at their last meal together or think of his mother? It's an unrecorded part of the narrative; we can only imagine what happened.

But McGovern's speculation might bring tremendous consolation to people trapped in various addictions, imprisoned, or victimized in the countless ways humans torture one another to know that Jesus endured what they do. He who was beauty, grace, freedom, and compassion chained to a filthy wall. He who had never hurt anyone feeling the raw bite of metal into his skin. He who had such clarity about his mission not knowing what horror the morning might bring. He entered deeply into the worst of being human.

Veneration of the Cross: People seemed drawn to the crucifix; to touch it lightly, cling to a hand, or kiss the feet. What is the compelling power of this instrument of death used by the Romans over two thousand years ago? As our pastor pointed out: It's not the cross; it's the body. Simply to revere the cross would be like honoring Martin Luther King, Jr., by hanging up a gun.

Father Richard Rohr describes the corpus: "Jesus' body is a standing icon of what humanity is doing and what God suffers 'with,' 'in,' and 'through' us. It is an icon of utter divine solidarity with our pain and our problems."[1]

Each person who approaches bears some kind of sorrow. Scratch the surface of any group, and you'll find the tragedies. In a family, a staff, on a work site, the stories of suffering run deep. Add in the veterans of Iraq or Afghanistan, the physical and mental aftermaths of war and the ripple effect on their families—an immense tide of suffering crashes at the foot of the crucifix. And there are millions of stories.

During the service this year, those who venerated the cross came close to the crucified Jesus to find meaning in their own burdens. Connecting their pain to his meant that they didn't suffer alone. Wave after wave of people in vast variety approached: the lovely couple whose daughter died last year in a freak accident, the vulnerable elderly who could barely bend to touch it, a woman battling cancer, the wife of an Iraq war veteran addicted to painkillers, an obese woman whose childhood hungers still drove her to eat, jeopardizing her health. The children were especially touching, quietly extending their thin arms, and perhaps whispering, "I'm sorry, Jesus, that you had to die like this." Knowing his magnificent courtesy, Jesus would somehow touch those who touched his cross.

---

[1] *Wondrous Encounters: Scripture for Lent* (Cincinnati: St. Anthony Messenger Press, 2011), 137.

QUESTION FOR REFLECTION OR DISCUSSION

- Reconsider the questions in the second paragraph of "Setting the Tone," above.

The Catholic Chorus

Teresa: A sister who celebrated her golden jubilee several years ago says, "Most of my friends are Catholic—that helps. I need to be in a ritualistic atmosphere, and my parish does fine ritual. I practice Buddhist meditation because it's in tune with the early Christian stance. I like the wonderful feminist theologians and Catholic scholars in a variety of fields. We don't neglect the intellectual part of faith. I also like the offshoots of the Catholic faith, lived with a few modifications. It's exciting that the church is still a foundation for vibrant developments."

Chapter 13

Easter

Sometimes it helps to separate the religious meaning of Easter from all the cultural accumulations. This happened experientially for me one year when Easter brought snow and sickness. Without lilies, bunnies, bonnets, egg hunts, pastels, or yellow marshmallow chicks, this was the acid test of the feast. In a friend's mountain home, sniffling, coughing, and watching dreary weather, would the message of resurrection still hold?

Indeed, it came powerfully, through a totally unexpected channel: clearing skies and sunlight gradually stroking the mountaintops. What had been gray fog parted to reveal luminous peaks emerging slowly. It echoed the absence and presence, hidden and revealed, hide-and-seek themes of this season. The resurrected Jesus may be unrecognized or invisible, but he is still with his friends.

If there had been musical accompaniment, those mountains streaked with sun would have invited the Hallelujah Chorus, belted loudly. The mountains unfurled banners of good news, with granite heavily grounded yet airily sweeping the skies. While it's not our traditional image, a healing sleep without coughing fit Easter nevertheless—joy unexpectedly found in the midst of sorrow. Brian Doyle calls it "the brilliant thrill of Easter, which insists on life defeating death, light defeating dark, hope defeating despair, and how mad a belief, how brave."[1]

If the concept of resurrection is too huge to grasp, we approach it with small steps. That year, it meant walking outdoors beside a river, breaking through ice, instead of huddling by the fire all day. Anyone who climbs mountains knows that having a clear destination directs every step along the way. So too, our belief in resurrection affects every moment on this side of eternity. In a world where we get colds, eat sandwiches, and endure traffic jams shimmers a hidden dimension. Easter is woven like a hopeful gold thread through all our experiences.

---

1 *Give Us This Day* (November 11, 2011), 6.

This Easter dimension happens because we believe that the news delivered to women at a tomb also comes to us. As we gradually grasp that message, it exerts a steady influence on every experience we have. We, like Thomas, learn to entertain doubts confidently, knowing them as gateways to deeper belief. When we bring Easter balm to the places of crushing disappointment, the grieving, bruised, and aching chambers of our hearts, resurrection recurs. Thomas Merton explains what we celebrate at Easter: "There is nothing lost that God cannot find again. Nothing dead that cannot live again in the presence of His Spirit. No heart so dark, so hopeless, that it cannot be enlightened and brought back to itself, warmed back to the life of charity."[2]

EASTER AS A VERB

Jesuit poet Gerard Manley Hopkins uses *easter* as an active verb, asking the risen Lord to "easter in us, be a dayspring to the dimness of us, be a crimson-cresseted east." The context is important here; this line is from "The Wreck of the Deutschland," a poem in which Hopkins struggles with the news that five Franciscan nuns have drowned in a storm at sea. We who are no strangers to such disasters recognize the situation he describes:

Hope had grown grey hairs,
Hope had mourning on.

If we deny such glumness, if we've never seen hope clothed in black, we fail to understand why Easter is such a gift. Perhaps it is only out of dark desperation that we can turn to the resurrection and fully appreciate the potential for Christ himself to "easter in us." Like the clueless disciples trudging to Emmaus, we ask him to "stay with us" (Lk 24:29).

That is our prayer in whatever dark trench we find ourselves. If we too have lost hope, enthusiasm, or even interest, it doesn't seem to bother him. Somehow, he rekindles the dormant spark so it becomes an inner flame. He gladly joins a long walk and conversation, winding it up, typically, with a meal.

The message is kept alive by a community that walks and eats together, shares stories and stakes everything on this one wild hope. We agree with the poet Alice Meynell, who writes in "Christ in the Universe" that our planet "bears, as chief treasure, one forsaken grave." Those who follow Jesus

---

[2] Thomas Merton, *The New Man* (New York: Farrar, Straus and Giroux, 1961), 241–42.

believe that he is our resurrection and life—not in some rosy heaven or distant future, but right here, right now.

Scripture scholar Luke Johnson explains that the Christian's memory of Jesus is not like that of a long ago lover who died and whose short time with us is treasured. It's rather like a lover who continues to live with the beloved in a growing, maturing relationship. Past memory is constantly affected by the continued experience of the other in the present. So the church's memory of Jesus is affected by his continuous and powerful presence. Jesus comes to life again and again, just as he did for Mary, Peter, and John that gray morning near the tomb.

Because of his life in us we can be vulnerable and weak in a world set on power and ambition. He brings intimacy to the lonely, peace to those in turmoil, strength to those weakened by illness. As he did during his life on earth, Jesus heals those in pain, welcomes those in exile, restores dignity to those in desperation, and comforts those who sorrow. He assures us all: "I created you for everlasting life. You are too precious to ever let you die. You will live forever." For the frightened, discouraged, hesitant person in each of us, Easter spells life, love, and hope.

Our belief may translate into small deeds: greeting the morning expectantly, offering someone a second chance, looking for the good in apparently bad news, or reading between the lines of disaster to find hidden promise. Easter belief explains why the funerals of the El Salvadoran martyrs were punctuated with applause and cries of "resurrexit!" Our belief in resurrection releases us from all that drains, demeans, and dehumanizes, liberating us into the glorious freedom of God's children.

Mark's original ending to the Easter story sounds so disheartening that later editors added a more upbeat conclusion. He wrote of women who "were terrified so they said nothing to anyone" (16:8). Rather than a "klunker," that may be an invitation. *We* must continue the story. As Dom Helder Camara of Brazil writes: "We Christians have no right to forget that we are not born to die; we are born to live. We must hold on to hope . . . since we have the deep certainty of being born for Easter."

News this good is best expressed in song. Some of the finest Easter music is Handel's "Messiah." Imagine a dynamic gospel choir, clothed in red robes. Its members sway, they clap, they sing full-throated. The orchestra adds brass, drums, and strings to energize the alleluias. It's traditional for the audience to stand for the Hallelujah Chorus in tribute to a splendid expression of the human spirit. On tiptoe, they applaud so intensely that the air rings with the clapping. It is a splendid image for the best news we could ever hear: "He is not here, but he has been raised."

QUESTIONS FOR REFLECTION OR DISCUSSION

- To appreciate the resurrection of Jesus, we must first appreciate the little resurrections in our own experience: sunny weather after a blizzard, health after illness, new energy in a project or relationship. Where have you met with experiences of resurrection?
- Do you have difficulty believing that the good news delivered to women at a tomb also comes to us? Why or why not?

THE CATHOLIC CHORUS

Alexia: Now a spiritual director, Alexia and her husband were active in lay movements for many years.

"I truly look forward to weekly mass, despite the priest who cracks inappropriate jokes at the most sacred moments. I also like how Catholic women make things happen. They're courageous enough to say, 'This needs change—or work. It's been with us forever, so now let's move into the twenty-first century.' Many Catholic lay people are quite active, and a number of priests encourage them, regardless of whether the bishop approves."

Chapter 14

The Parish Nucleus

A vibrant parish is surely one of the best things about being Catholic. I'll describe two examples, starting with Most Precious Blood Parish in Denver, my home base. I'm outrageously grateful for it and fortunate to draw from such an energy-giving well. It stands on a continuum of parishes. Some may be more vibrant, others less engaging. Imagine now that you're visiting there . . .

Before you even get inside, you know what the parish's focus is. A big truck on the parking lot is busily accepting donations for the St. Vincent de Paul Society. As people unload chairs and tables, china and clothing, they know it will find its way to someone who really needs it. In the vestibule sales of fair-trade coffee are brisk. On other weekends crafts to benefit El Salvador or breads for a youth-group trip are sold. A plethora of activities benefits many organizations with similar missions.

Inside there's happy commotion: a broad age range, a spectrum of economic groups, many ethnicities. The atmosphere is welcoming; people can participate as much or as little as they want. The music somehow manages to be both robust and soothing, and often a child will dance in the aisle. Many parishioners volunteer to make sure liturgy is both reverent and relevant. Homilies unfailingly contain an insightful nugget to reflect on further that week—and enough humor to make the message palatable.

An atmosphere of anticipation pervades the church. Quiet conversations and hugs among friends carry the undertone that something important is about to happen here. For an hour a week no one has to worry about appearance, IQ, or bank account. Liturgy is the great equalizer: all do essentially the same thing, singing, worshiping, and chuckling when the homily is funny. It's one of the few places in our culture where we're not judged on *success*.

Internal disputes that once raged quiet with time; even those on opposite ends of the political or theological spectrum enjoy coffee and donuts together after mass. Over the forty years I've belonged here, we've had many pastors, ranging from superb and life-changing to mediocre or pathetic. Regardless of the leadership, a core group continues. It's a place with easy forgiveness and broad tolerance. Mistakes are accepted because everyone has made them. We go forth each week feeling happier about being human, renewed to serve our individual sectors.

Our current pastor, Pat Dolan, encourages questions and challenges, because if all walk in lock step, in smiling agreement on *everything*, how can we grow? He also comments frequently about the community's ease with human failings. Once during the Easter season a young soloist was left hanging when she sang an extra "Alleluia" after the rest of the choir and instruments stopped. As if to prove the general health of this group, she laughed, shrugged, and sat down. No teeth-grinding embarrassment, no exaggerating her mistake. Our pastor, a musician himself, delighted in this minor error, admitting that he'd probably made every gaffe in the musical book.

One year, just before school began, the parish parking lots were resealed with tar. Due to unusually hot temperatures, the tar didn't set. Staff, faculty, and 350 children trouped through it, collecting plenty on their shoes and depositing it on the carpet. As Father Pat wrote in the bulletin, "A small child staring at its shoe with an expression somewhere between revulsion and pure wonder seems momentarily stuck to gooey strings of tar. However, it's the type of inconvenient annoyance that might still bring laughter." And the laughter ricocheted around the building when one of the teachers brought a treat: licorice. A sign beside it invited everyone to join in the "tar festival." It was a classic case of trial turned to triumph, a chance for gratitude despite annoyance. Father Pat concluded, "We're gifted with a parking lot! Children! And volunteers to clean up the mess!"

Not to idealize: This parish has conflicts, gossip and worries like any other group of human beings. But it has consistently tried to avoid navel gazing and instead to focus on those who need help. Some people cook for the battered-women's shelter; others support a sister parish in El Salvador; others collect food, school supplies, and Christmas gifts for the needy; still others counsel the jobless or grieving.

A traveling homeless shelter visits every two months. An effort with many neighboring churches, the Interfaith Hospitality Network offers shelter to many families as well as nutritious meals and partnerships with other non-profits that address specific needs. The work of one hundred volunteers transforms the parish center into separate living spaces with clean sheets and privacy. Parents from the parish bring their children to socialize with the homeless children over evening games. The focus is on getting to know one another as individuals, not faceless categories.

Not all is charity. Many events buoy the spirits of those who make their spiritual home here: an eighty-voice chorus singing the Passion in Holy

Week; a dance performance; a St. Patrick's Day dinner that benefits battered women; a marathon run or carnival; a women's choir for Father's Day and a men's choir for Mother's Day; a parish retreat; moms', seniors', and men's groups; weekly sessions for adult education that stimulate creative thinking.

During Lent and in autumn many people sign up for "One Parish, One Book," reading and discussing a volume that enhances their faith. Traditional devotions aren't neglected; a Way of the Cross might precede a soup supper. For January's Week of Christian Unity the parish joins with other denominations in the neighborhood to pray, sing, and hear scripture together.

While not all parishes have the resources, talented musicians, and gifted homilist we do, they too live as "brothers and sisters in the Lord." A friend living in a rural town described her parish, "The musicians try but get off key, the people croak, the homilist bores, but we love one another."

What makes a parish great? Am I unusually lucky to belong to an excellent one, or are there common threads? Paul Wilkes explored this topic more thoroughly in *Excellent Catholic Parishes: The Guide to Best Places and Practices.*[1] My research, on the other hand, is admittedly informal. But when I visit a fine parish to give a retreat or workshops there, I have a clear intuition: this is one of the best.

That struck me on my arrival at Holy Family in South Pasadena, California, Archdiocese of Los Angeles. The massive ficus tree in the central courtyard looks like the tree of life. Indeed, beneath its broad boughs unfold numerous activities like a Sunday welcome center or a weekend family fair. Similar to many parishes, it hosts a school, liturgies, grief ministry, centering-prayer group, a soup kitchen that feeds three hundred people weekly, RCIA, choirs, youth groups, book clubs—the usual suspects.

What seems more unique here is the richness of many threads seeming to blend seamlessly into one mystical body. (Although I don't stay in a parish long enough to see its darker side, it's safe to assume that even the finest parishes have their faults. I like being the temporary visitor who can become the enthusiastic cheerleader.) What is remarkable is how people of vast diversity—different ages, ethnic backgrounds, educational levels, socioeconomic groups—can become one. I hesitate to use the overused word *family,* but it seems to fit here. In a larger world plagued by alienation and loneliness, this faith community shares a story and images that bind them deeper than superficial ties.

---

[1] Mahwah, NJ: Paulist Press, 2001.

At Holy Family the operative theme is "A Community of Beloved Disciples." It all began when Monsignor Clement Connolly, who served as pastor for twenty-five years and is now pastor emeritus, attended a seminar with Father Raymond Brown, the illustrious Johannine scholar. Brown had long taught that the Beloved Disciple, named four times in John's Gospel (13:23; 19:26; 20:1–10; 21:1–25), is deliberately unnamed because he represents all of us. We all stand as close to Jesus as the one who reclined beside him at the Last Supper. As the parish website says, "All those who follow Jesus seeking discipleship are in fact beloved."

Monsignor Connolly often uses the theme that each of us is completely beloved in his homilies and in one-on-one spiritual direction. Consequently, this understanding has become embedded in the Holy Family faith tradition. Visible signs are a statue of the Beloved Disciple commissioned for the parish's one-hundredth anniversary and placed in a niche on the church's south wall. A beautiful song and prayer composed for that event are used at the opening of parish meetings.

Parish Life Director Cambria Smith adds, "We, as a Community of Beloved Disciples, participate in the extraordinary blessing of God's continuous gift of grace by reflecting God's love in the world." It might all seem like beautiful rhetoric if it weren't so carefully put into practice through many facets.

The ideal translates to the real as a young woman searching for a parish "where someone knows my name" joins the Women's Connection at Holy Family. Many years later she recalls how at a time when she felt unsure, they "wrapped me in their embrace, almost like a womb." She probably didn't know St. Augustine's image for the church as a womb, holding, warming, and nurturing the newcomer. But from her personal experience she reached the same comparison. She tried several parish ministries and Bible study, and now a larger community calls her by name.

Furthermore, Holy Family has the courage to implement a pioneering model of leadership. When the Irish pastor foresaw his retirement, the parish sought a lay parish life director. There are fewer than one hundred of these in the United States, but surely it's a hopeful direction for the future. One requirement must be a priest secure enough in the knowledge of being beloved to cede his power, office, and multiple responsibilities to a lay man or lay woman. That's what happened here. Cambria Smith is a dynamo who has already been celebrated in Michael Novak's and William Simon's *Living the Call: An Introduction to the Lay Vocation*.[2] One of her many gifts is outreach to parishioners, inviting their talents into the service of the community.

---

[2] New York: Encounter Books, 2011.

For instance, she asks them to consider supporting Mission Haiti: "Our parish commitment to Haiti, the poorest nation in the Western Hemisphere, is a beautiful response of solidarity with the poor and vulnerable in our world." This translates to large amounts of religious art being sent to Haitian churches demolished by the earthquake as well as an annual collection.

Because the parish has a long history of lay involvement and is a complex place, a three-year process led to the decision that Cambria's leadership would fit better than a priest appointed for five years. Her background in finances, personnel, and spirituality has suited her for such diverse duties as leading prayer services, visiting parishioners in the hospital, and bringing together diverse cultural groups. Novak and Simon comment on one event: "Between the roasted pig provided by the Tongan community, the Indonesian dances and the religious camaraderie, the occasion was a success." One measure of the parish's activity: ninety ministries, a hundred staff, and seven masses from Saturday through Sunday evening.

The liturgy gives flesh to Denis McBride's words: "At a solemn Mass, after the priest incenses the altar and bread and wine, he then bows to the people and incenses them. Where else but in the Christian liturgy are people reverenced and incensed for who they are? . . . *In this place* people's identity is not dependent on what work they do or on what career advances they have secured; rather, they are reverenced for who they are in being children of God."[3]

Most Catholics, I suspect, feel their first loyalty toward their family and parish before any larger systems. When the events of a week are dispiriting, the parish gives a community, a place, and an inspiration to focus on "whatever is true, whatever is honorable, whatever is just, whatever is pure, whatever is pleasing, whatever is commendable, if there is any excellence and if there is anything worthy of praise, think about these things" (Phil 4:8). If our days have been thorny, the liturgy redirects our gaze to the roses.

The letters of St. Paul recognized the autonomy of each early Christian community. He also encouraged them to think of their unity as the body of Christ.

Much as Paul may have wanted to assert his authority over early faith-based groups, especially when they got cantankerous, he couldn't do it because of Jesus' model. Jesus always knew when dealing with adults to respect their ideas and honor their inherent dignity. Never in the gospels does he say, "Do it because I tell you."

---

[3] *Waiting on God* (Liguori, MO: Liguori Press, 2004), 53.

A final gesture captures the best parish spirit: An older woman hugging an adolescent at the sign of peace finishes with a hand lingering tenderly on his cheek. Asked if the young man was her grandson, she replied, "I don't know who he is, but he sat next to me in our church."

QUESTIONS FOR REFLECTION OR DISCUSSION

- Do you have a favorite parish? If so, describe it.
- What do you long for in a parish?

A Catholic Chorus

Sarah: Highly successful in a financial career, Sarah joined the Catholic Church over twenty years ago, volunteered at her parish in many capacities, and now sings in the choir. "I became Catholic when my husband saw the community at our local parish and said, 'This is what we're missing.' I've come to appreciate it now—a community that survives together through all the changes in leadership, liturgy, and life. I come for the camaraderie—not necessarily the homily. And I've tried many different kinds of ministry. Where else can you try different things in a supportive place and walk away without a problem? There aren't a lot of places in life where you can do that, definitely not in your job!

"Mass is my foundation week after week, no matter what else happens during that week. Spirituality ebbs and flows for me. Even when I don't feel very spiritual, I still go—and maybe something touches me, brings it back. I went to a parish in Laramie, Wyoming, to what turned out to be a Latin mass. Clearly someone was touched by that—not me—but the church was filled. I disagree with a lot of the dogma and hierarchical stances, but I can still be part of a community that allows huge diversity. How can you not allow diversity if you're truly following the teachings of Christ? Is it about the rules or the body of Christ? That applies to clergy too—how can you get the best quality if you exclude so many kinds of people? Is our loyalty to the institution or to Christ?"

Chapter 15

Removing Shoes

The Holy Grounds of the Retreat House

While the sacramental imagination sees all ground as holy, retreat houses deserve special mention for their sacred role in Catholic life. Around the world stretches a network of these centers; some are located on spectacular coastlines, harbors or mountain ranges, while others nestle in Midwestern cornfields. Whatever the setting, the work is similar. Furnished with a stretch of empty time, simple meals, and solitary space, people can concentrate on the real work of their lives: growing closer to God. They don't remain indefinitely (staffs are suspicious of "retreat junkies" who come too often). Instead, they return renewed to family and work, inspired as if by the Benedictine motto, "always we begin again." Those outside concerns are primary, so important that they deserve the best self, not one who's exhausted and functioning on minimal inner resources.

It's another aspect of Catholicism that's counter-cultural. "What?" stolid bureaucrats might protest. "You mean retreatants aren't *working*? They've abandoned their families, homes, usual niches? How *dare* they be so irresponsible?"

Exactly. They've entered what some writers call *liminal space,* that threshold where humans stand alone before God without any of the familiarities that normally shore them up. They abandon the usual routines of comfortable homes: cocktails, television, small talk, puttering in the garden, baseball games. In a small room, a chapel, or lots of acreage in which to walk, they meet themselves—and God.

In so doing, they follow a long line. Early Christian fathers and mothers of the church retired to the desert. St. Benedict, fearing the collusion of church and state in the Roman Empire, withdrew to a cave. There he began his *Rule* with a key question: Am I fully alive?

St. Francis tossed the silken garments provided by his wealthy merchant father at the feet of the bishop, and fled naked to transform the dandy he'd once been into the troubadour of Lady Poverty.

The dynamic is the same for Benedict, Francis, or a retreatant today. They step into apparent emptiness and harvest abundant treasure.

Silence is hard to find in a noisy world of traffic jams and TV jingles, iPods and chattering conversations. Simply to sink into the quiet, even for an extrovert, can be rich. God can speak; humans can listen. How obvious it seems; how rarely we do it.

Even if we don't achieve tremendous insights or become startlingly better people, we have at least taken one step away from pettiness. We have tried to look beneath the turbulent surface of our lives to the depth, the serenity of God and the saints.

It's heartening to see retreat houses often filling with students of high school age. Retreats are a high priority for Catholic schools; even the seniors get days off from SATs and college applications to tend their core selves. Learning to pray and dialogue about matters of substance merits as much concentrated effort as the study of physics or chemistry. The hope must be that introducing the young to the retreat is like handing on a family heirloom, a precious part of our tradition. And the young respond enthusiastically, taking seriously their time apart, valuing it as an essential component of their educations.

In *A Portrait of the Artist as a Young Man,* James Joyce describes a "preached retreat" that blew death and terror into the souls of the young. The horrors of hell were vividly portrayed to shame them. Overwrought rhetoric was designed to convince them of their own sinful misery. But what once terrified James Joyce is no longer the only format. Now the presenters may be a mother-daughter team, small groups working collaboratively, or individuals with a director.

RING LAKE RANCH

The setting may be as broadly ecumenical as Ring Lake Ranch near Dubois, Wyoming. While superb speakers present each evening, they aren't the most important part of the program. First priority is attentiveness to God's creation through leisure time for canoeing, horseback riding, hiking, reflecting. No speaker or book could rival the powerful message of Wind River mountains, lakes, waterfalls, boulders, and streams. People hiking or riding together discover that one is the canon of Portland Episcopal cathedral; another is a United Methodist or Lutheran minister; another is a Franciscan nun; yet another a Hawaiian psychologist.

The common denominator goes deeper than religious tradition, or the lack of one. It's a shared reverence for natural beauty, an interest in spirituality, a joy in impossibly starry skies. People ask the right questions: not "what denomination are you?" but "where's your center?" "Have you gotten out of balance?" "What unique gift do you bring to the people of God?"

Optional morning prayer usually consists of a psalm and a reading from Brian Swimme, Rumi, or Ed Hayes. Reflections before meals are broadly ecumenical, usually geared to seeing the reality around us—not what we construct in our heads, but what's actually there. People who laugh somewhat guiltily at their "shadow" side recognize it as the extravagant flights of fancy, the intense worry, the "what if?" speculation that drains energy and devours time. Shifting focus to the snow-frothed mountaintop gilded in twilight or the sun-warmed rocks beside the pounding brook places people in a long spiritual tradition of attentiveness. Invoking Christ's presence in the day, participants leave uplifted, open to whatever blessings might come:

May the peace of the Lord Christ go with you wherever he may send you;
May he guide you through the wilderness, protect you through the storm;
May he bring you home rejoicing at the wonders he has shown you;
May he bring you home rejoicing once again into our doors.[1]

Many come to retreats in need of healing. During even the brief initial introductions, the wounds surface: a cancer diagnosis, the recent death of a spouse or child, a betrayal, job loss, difficult teenager, or the strain of caregiving. For those with more ordinary problems, the poet Jane Hirshfield sums up what happens in her poem "The Promise":

It was not any awakening of the large, not so much as that,
only a stepping back from the petty.[2]

CHRIST THE KING RETREAT HOUSE

While the setting is more intentionally Catholic than Ring Lake Ranch, Christ the King Retreat House in Schuyler, Nebraska, welcomes all denominations, and it's not unusual to have a walking ecumenical movement gathered there for a day or a weekend. Unexpectedly located in the middle of Nebraska, founded by German Benedictines who escaped Hitler, it's a blessed sanctuary that considers spiritual need a better focus than denominational difference.

---

[1] "A Morning Prayer [December 2 et al.]," *Common Prayer: A Liturgy for Ordinary Radicals* (Grand Rapids, MI: Zondervan, 2010), 52, among others.

[2] *After* (New York: Harper, 2007), 46.

Founded to support the order's missionary activity around the world, it is a treasure house of art from many countries, elegantly displayed in spacious corridors and public spaces made beautiful with archways. Set on a small lake, the library or scriptorum is warm with a fireplace and a Peruvian sculpture of the Last Supper. To anyone who relishes study, or simply quiet reading, it is a haven for the heart.

I once spent a graced weekend there with Julian of Norwich, the first known female writer in English. She fits squarely within the best of Catholicism, never judgmental, never seeing God as punitive. A fourteenth-century mystic who is deeply reassuring, her most famous mantra is probably, "all will be well." While she admits that sin is an essential part of the pattern, it does not have the power to destroy that essential wellness. Not relying on previous texts, Julian explores the divine in order to understand human living—and addresses her writing not only to theologians but to everyone. She also encourages us with the conviction that God could never reject what God has made: "So are we spirit and flesh, clothed head to toe in the goodness of God" (44).[3]

Her God is endlessly forgiving: "out of his great courtesy, he never censures us" (61). She portrays a God intimately involved with creation, whose work doesn't stop: "Behold, I never withdraw my arms from my work" (50). It is hard to imagine Julian's God ever frowning, excluding, criticizing, or condemning: "The merciful gaze of his face ranged over all the world" (110). Her prayer never berates herself as some self-flagellating saints do; instead, she asks, "Courteous Lord, teach me the extent of your delight in me" (190). It would go a long way toward making peace with all the different arenas of our lives if we could come to see them not as burdens but as gift and delight.

All our petty anxieties and concerns seem erased by her broad view. She says when all mysteries are unveiled, we won't say, "if only things were different," but, "Whatever is, is good." She even sees God as thanking us for our service and labor (211).

Like St. Ignatius Loyola, who blessed our deep desires, Julian sees Jesus as their source: "I endow you with longing; I am the endless completion of all desiring" (144). Julian's prayer is for oneness with God: "Courteous God, be the foundation of my being. May I sit in you in true rest, stand in you in sure strength, and be rooted in you in endless love" (136).

---

[3] Richard Chilson, *All Will Be Well: Based on the Classic Spirituality of Julian of Norwich* (Notre Dame, IN: Ave Maria Press, 1995). Page numbers for the quotations from this volume appear in the text.

The combination of lovely setting and Julian's inspiration restored my droopy spirits. Or, as she would say to God, "[Your] beloved Son had restored to this city its noble beauty through his tremendous labor" (109).

That weekend at the retreat house inspired me to write this poem:

St. Benedict Hoists the Sky

For the Priory of Christ the King, Schuyler, Nebraska

Poised between an eastern edge
of fuchsia and a gauzy moon,
his statue a bronze slash
through crimsoning sunrise.
Open stance of trust, arms wide
as prairie or hawk wingspan,
both hands reach into mystery.

Glass-blown clouds net
wisps of scarlet. His thrust
into the future repels despair.
Sculpture infused with might
shouts, we're children of infinity
enveloped in networks beyond.
Each day has reasons for joy.

The saints: rule keepers, or
dazzled, amazed delighters?
Coiled spring of exuberance,
toss of burgundy banner,
surge of brass band pulsing
through tawny cornfields,
tickling hidden critters.

Lake laps his feet
washed in pastels.
He floats at ease, blessing
this hospitable sanctuary of
spacious arches, art, chant,
Kenyan Madonnas, long
monastic line, Benedictine beauty.

QUESTIONS FOR REFLECTION OR DISCUSSION

- Do you have a special place like those described where you can find quiet and refresh your spirit? If so, what does it add to your spiritual life? If not, do you miss it?
- Of all the quotations from Julian of Norwich, which was your favorite?

A Catholic Chorus

Jon: Trained as an engineer, Jon worked for NASA, then eventually became a Merton scholar and priest. Teaching comparative religions in an ecumenical setting at Naropa Institute in Boulder, Colorado, helped him clarify his own stance. Widely read and articulate, he was a font of wisdom throughout our three-hour interview.

"Smiling serenely, he says, "The best part of being Catholic is living in paradox. It's the creative climate of our transformation. We think paradox must be resolved. Fear keeps us from living there, but if we're not there—personally, communally, ecclesially—we follow our own designs. That's risky, since we don't always stand 100 percent in line with God's designs. The greatest risk we take in life is faith—we could be wrong!

"Does God exist or does our need for God create God? Can we live with the paradox of the unanswered question? We're still evolving—it's not like we've arrived! We need to know our history, not try to define any paradox in isolation. We've been here before, got through it before.

"Another great thing about being Catholic is we have a fine tradition with diverse spiritualities articulated and lived out by many people. Being grounded in one tradition enables one to explore paradoxes in dialogue with other traditions, to better understand our own and God's universal call. Knowing where we stand, we can read others' stories and find the commonalities in them.

"There's no evidence of diverse religions meeting as they developed, but the parallels among them are striking. That's why the Vatican II document Gaudium et Spes *said 'the church rejects nothing of what is true and holy in these religions.'*

"Pope John XXIII was fearless because he had nothing to lose. He was the 'lame duck pope' and from that fertile ground grew Vatican II.

"Our weakness is the ground of holiness. Our wounds are the door to grace. One can't truly know hope until one sees how like despair it is. On Good Friday, Jesus doesn't foresee Easter.

"People who stay in the church are the martyrs of today. The institution can diminish prophets like Yves Congar or Teilhard de Chardin. Teilhard could've walked away when silenced—he had enough money. He models how to live creatively and authentically in our own time.

"I've been gifted to experience intercultural and religious diversity. Even within the different rites of the Catholic Church, some allow married clergy.

"Difference doesn't necessarily mean division. Uniformity doesn't guarantee unity. The great need now is forums for dialogue, and if we wait for the institution to create those, it will never happen. We are the body of Christ, but we're dividing it, fracturing the body just as in the fraction rite of the mass. The first rule of any institution is self-preservation—but at what cost?

"The more we try to withdraw from mystery, and control life, [the more] we diminish who we are—the people of God first, before anything structural. When we lose sight of the mystery of the integrating Spirit working in the body of Christ, we wind up forming camps. We lose the holistic vision of Lumen Gentium *and wind up with war and violence.*

"We must also remember the vast breadth of people the Vatican speaks to, many of them hungry. Only in Europe and North America do we have the luxury of drinking coffee and discussing theology. On the ladder of human needs, people must first satisfy the basic ones—food, shelter, and so forth. We're born with a need for security, love, and esteem—and we'll die with the same needs. [These parallel Jesus's three temptations in the desert.]

"Finally, the best thing about being Catholic is the companions—from scripture, the prophets, Jesus, the desert dwellers, Benedict and monastic traditions, the saints, one another."

Part III

The Company We Keep

Introduction

The Breadth of the Umbrella

Every book, film, or play must have its cast of characters, or it would have no human interest. The Catholic Church is no different; one of its best features is the company of believers. Another term for this is the *communion of saints,* in which neither time nor distance creates barriers to presence. Or as Father Michael Himes jokes, "It's like voting in Cook County. Death doesn't disqualify."

Some people marvel that the variety that has led to splinter groups in other denominations has somehow been contained under the vast Catholic roof or umbrella. Not that it isn't a precarious balancing act at times; undeniably, the church is strained with tensions. When tempers fray, it's good to remember that we have more in common than our differences might at first suggest. Diversity pops up golden as dandelions in the lawn and keeps the Catholic community alive and interesting.

What I love about the church is similar to what I love about my family: the quirkiness, humor, generosity, and special traits of individual members. I also love who we are as a whole: watching the interplay among siblings, the rivalries among children that have transformed into the deep respect and concern of young adults for one another; relishing the particular energy that happens when we all sit down for a meal together. Did I condone young children's misdeeds? Of course not, but I regard them now in the larger context of how much they do right. If they have learned from their mistakes, then those were necessary stepping stones in the process of maturing.

So with the church. I hope that some of the current controversies are necessary milestones as we grow into the healed wholeness of Christ. "Tooting one's own horn" was frowned upon by my Irish grandmother, but sometimes it's important—especially given the morale crisis that has affected the church since the pedophilia scandals. Without apology, we must cling tenaciously to the good when the bad news seems so overwhelming.

Early in his career Barack Obama, skeptical of religion, saw too much dissension between Catholics and Protestants working for the poor in Chicago. But his attitude gradually changed. He describes a meeting with the Altgeld community, where he was touched by compassion springing from faith and by the prayer for "the courage to turn things around." As his experience broadened, his perspective shifted. He appreciated the sense of "witness, frustration, and hope" in the Catholic community—in contrast to the grim contempt for community norms in violent gangs.[1]

Within this section thrive people who might not agree on any subject except the core doctrines of their faith. More traditional sisters might not approve of my friend the nun who savors hot tubs. But the whole spectrum, Sunday after Sunday, in every parish, stands together to recite the same Creed. The participants do not disagree on core beliefs like the divinity and humanity of Christ, the resurrection, the Eucharist. Crossing the threshold of the church, a widely varied group becomes one people, singing one song, praying with one voice, called to become the mystical body of Christ. As *Environment and Art in Catholic Worship* states, "The most powerful experience of the sacred is found in the celebration and the persons celebrating, that is, in the action of the assembly" (no. 29). Or, as St. Teresa of Avila wrote in the sixteenth century:

Christ has no body but yours,
No hands, no feet on earth but yours.

A similar passage from Exodus 17:8–13 recounts that as long as Moses held his arms up, the Israelites triumphed over their enemies in battle. But his arms grew tired, so Aaron and Hur supported them, one on each side. The Hebrews won the battle, but more helpful to us now is the metaphor. How many people uphold the work of Christ, how many hands contribute to what Catholics call the mystical body, Jesus' presence in our world?

Dorothy Day, working in the squalor of New York City, had a unique understanding of that presence. She wrote in her diary: "'He was a man so much like other men that it took the kiss of a Judas to single him out,' [François] Mauriac wrote. He was like that man in the pew beside me. He was as like him as his brother. He was his brother. And I felt Christ in that man beside me and loved him."[2]

---

[1] Quoted in James Kloppenberg, *Reading Obama* (Princeton, NJ: Princeton University Press, 2011), 200–201.

[2] Quoted in Robert Ellsberg, ed., *The Duty of Delight: The Diaries of Dorothy Day* (Milwaukee, WI: Marquette University Press, 2008), 38.

Chapter 16

"Glorious Nobodies"

The Communion of Saints

They are not found among the rulers.
But they maintain the fabric of the world.

—Sirach 38:33–34

Snow shovelers, flight attendants, phlebotomists, kindergarten aides, car mechanics, postal workers, lawn mowers, cooks, farmers, computer technicians, produce managers, librarians, garbage collectors: they make a lovely litany for the feast of All Saints.

Sometimes when I get depressed about the folks at the top—the greed-driven executives, the hypocritical leaders, the unethical actions of the supposedly "best and brightest," I like to think of Tim.

Tim's job wasn't prestigious. He worked as an aide at a retirement center where my eighty-four-year-old friend Cathey lives. Sometimes I pick her up for a lecture or a concert, because she craves stimulation and loves to get out. One cold morning when I arrived, Tim greeted me at the door. "Cathey's got only a light jacket. Do you think she'll be warm enough?" he asked with concern. "She's so excited about going—I styled her hair." Cathey emerged several minutes later, glowing. I complimented her hair while Tim retrieved a heavier coat. As he waved us off, I thought no parent had sent a child to prom with more tenderness or pride.

Do we think of Tim as a saint? Probably not. Aren't saints the folks with lush capes and sculpted haloes, glowing through stained glass? Even in martyrdom their hair is perfectly coiffed, not one brocade thread of one sleeve askew. They are *never* overweight, late, anxious, or irritable. But such an image does a great disservice to the reality. When we put the saints on a pedestal, we're off the hook. If they were perfect, we don't need to imitate them.

The reading for this feast, the beatitudes, certainly contradicts the idea of distance. In Luke 6, Jesus stands "on a level place," in a posture of equality with people who were probably sweaty, diseased, and smelly. They would've chortled at the idealized portraits, but they were united in their desire to be near Jesus. Why did they jostle one another to be close, longing for his touch? Daniel O'Leary explains, "There was an attractiveness about the reality of Jesus' company, about the way he looked and listened to people, that they simply fell in love with."[1]

Perhaps the saints, then, are people so drawn to Christ's vibrant energy that they mirror him, just as long-married couples begin to resemble each other. They proclaim what Christ looks like—and there are infinite varieties on the theme.

The statue of St. Benedict at the Priory of Christ the King once startled me into new realizations about sanctity. The saint's arms are spread wide as the surrounding prairie. He looks up happily, joyous and inclusive. The sunrise seems like a fuchsia banner he tosses into the sky with glad abandon. His followers carry on his heritage with reverent liturgy and a beautiful retreat center.

St. Benedict changes my image of the saints as dogged followers of rules. Maybe, instead, they are dazzled delighters who walk through life amazed at God's wonders. Instead of hounding people about their flaws, they rejoice with gratitude at what is. St. Benedict advised, "Listen with the ear of your heart." The saints are the people alert to those hints, eagerly following the Creator's traces through their days.

Elizabeth Johnson names this the feast of "'anonymous,' whom the world counts as nobodies and whom the church, too, has lost track of but who are held in the embrace of God who loses not one." As Johnson explains, holiness isn't due to anything human beings have done or earned. Instead, it results from God drawing near to us with an infinite and contagious graciousness. She defines the communion of saints: "This is a people shaped by a profound relationship with the Holy One that acts like a deep spring of creative power at their very core."[2] In exalting human beings, we are in fact praising God. For this reason Paul addresses all the early Christians as "saints," even when he gets frustrated with their angry feuding.

We can't define "holy" people as "closer to God" if God is everywhere. When I gave a talk on this theme, a woman in the audience protested. "I was taught that only the priests and sisters are holy," she said. "What kind of work do you do?" I asked. "I volunteer as a catechist and help women in the homeless shelter get their GEDs," she replied. Then a wonderful

---

1 "Power of Real Presence," *The Tablet* (May 2009), 11-14.

2 *Friends of God and Prophets* (New York: Continuum, 1999), 250, 56.

eruption poured forth from the members of the audience: "What could be more holy than *that*?" they asked in a splendid demonstration of the community's power to teach. The lights that came on in the woman's face could've brightened the whole convention hall.

Mark 12:28–34 records a significant conversation between Jesus and a scribe. We're inclined to boo at this name, because we're conditioned to see scribes and Pharisees as the villains of the Gospels, so hell-bent on enforcing rules that they miss the Messiah. But this encounter is different. What begins in a dispute ends in a compliment. "When Jesus saw that he answered wisely, he said to him, 'You are not far from the kingdom of God'" (v. 34). Later writers (Luke and Matthew) omitted that line because they didn't want "the enemy" looking so good. Mark may have come closer to understanding Jesus, who delighted in goodness wherever he found it—even among the supposedly clueless.

Along those inclusive lines, it is comforting to know the infinite variety of paths to sainthood. From what we know of canonized saints with feast days, we can infer a lot about the anonymous saints who share the feast November 1. Some, like Thomas Beckett, seem catapulted there by the choices of others: the king who made his old friend head of the church in England. King Henry never suspected that Becket's loyalty would be given to God instead. For others like Thérèse of Lisieux, it's a slow, reflective process; they spend lots of time in prayer and reflection. Courteously and generously, they then share their mystic insights with the rest of us on the same path.

Others, like Frances Cabrini, are doers; they don't have time for long retreats or meditations. Prayer is almost always an important part of their work, infusing it with energy and compassion. But for the most part, their holiness is expressed in work with the poor, action for peace or social justice, or creating art, literature or music. Cabrini once asked God, "Give me a heart as big as the universe!" God must've answered, "OK."

Some come to God thinking (Thomas Aquinas, Edith Stein) or teaching (Charles Borromeo), others cooking (Martha, patron of chefs) or writing poetry (John of the Cross), some gardening (Rose of Lima), painting (Blessed Fra Angelico), or acting on stage (Pelagia). Imagine a heavenly deck, where from adjoining rocking chairs the saints admire the view. St. Teresa of Avila compares her interior castle to the celestial architecture. St. Elizabeth Ann Seton relaxes because her work is done; her many children are fed and educated. St. Ignatius leads an imaginative reflection, while St. Hildegard of Bingen sings an original tune.

Within our offices, classrooms, and homes are future versions of these great saints. We want to continue honoring that variety. Would the genius of Francis have flourished in the mold of Dominic? How unhappy Damien of Molokai would have been placed into the anchorage of St. Julian of Norwich. Katherine McAuley and Katharine Drexel couldn't have done their unique work in a cloister.

To anyone familiar with the saints' different personality types and stories, it's consoling to know that even someone as wacky as oneself can reach the ultimate goal of human life. The most highly improbable characters arrive in heaven. As the mystic Gabrielle Bossis wrote, "Don't think that a saint must look saintly in the eyes of humans. Saints have an outer nature, but it is the inner nature that counts. There is a fruit whose rough—even thorny—skin gives no inkling of its sweet and juicy taste. That is how it is for my saints. Their value is in their hearts."[3]

Perhaps we should celebrate this feast by looking more appreciatively at those around us, saints in disguise or in progress. There we'll find proof of Thomas Merton's conviction that being a saint means being ourselves. I tried this approach at the Mexican restaurant down the street, which has an assembly-line approach to building burritos. The women behind the counter load on beans and guacamole, sour cream, and cheese. It's the repetitive kind of work that would drive me up the wall within two hours, but the women are unfailingly gracious. They smile as they ladle on salsa with a generous hand, and we communicate with our eyes more than words. Their grandmothers, presiding over steamy stoves, may have taught them that food prepared with love warms the soul as well as the body.

Was that the glimmer of a halo along the line? Could those drab uniforms be the garments of holiness? Maybe there's more than fajitas in the making here. Stand back and admire—saints in the works!

QUESTIONS FOR REFLECTION OR DISCUSSION

- Why do we do the saints a disservice by putting them on a pedestal?
- In the vast communion of saints, canonized and un-, do you have a favorite? Describe this person.

A Catholic Chorus

Keisha: "After Vatican II, the church has grown large enough and flexible enough, that there are many options. If the Rosary isn't your thing, you can diversify. There are enough Sunday and daily masses that surely one will suit your style. Catholicism is the General Motors of religion!"

---

[3] Quoted in Robert Ellsberg, *Blessed among All Women* (New York: Crossroad, 2005), 120.

Chapter 17

A People Ahead of Their Time

I am a conference junkie. Because I've given talks at various parish, diocesan, and national events for the last twelve years, people often ask, "So, what do you see, traveling around the country?" It's probably a skewed perspective, flying in on Friday night, speaking most of Saturday, then returning to the airport Sunday. Sometimes a longer retreat or workshop gives me the chance to know people at a deeper level and communicate over a longer period of time. That kind of experience makes it harder to say goodbye, but is the exception, not the rule.

So much travel. What does it teach? Given the breadth of the action in a truly Catholic culture—from Asians in Seattle to Cubans in Miami, from Filipinos in Las Vegas to Latinos in Lubbock, any sweeping generalization sounds suspect. With that caveat comes a firmly optimistic read. For the most part, catechetical activity isn't generating headlines, but it speaks loud and clear of a robust faith community. In the old cliche, reports of the church's demise, at least in this arena, are exaggerated.

Come along for an imaginative tour of conferences around the country. Most events, whether in Milwaukee or Monterey, tend to be as similar as the Gap stores at the local mall. The folding chairs for a keynote in the elementary or high-school gym, the breakouts in classrooms, are sometimes upgraded to hotels or convention centers.

Whatever the site, the spirit is familiar; the planners generously invest abundant time in the details of preparation. On the day itself, hard-working people give up a Saturday to gain personal inspiration or learn techniques of better teaching. The frequent singing of "The Summons" at the opening prayer service is appropriate; participants have responded wholeheartedly to a sometimes inconvenient, often mysterious, but always compelling call.

Mostly women, but with a heartening, growing contingent of men, they huddle together over boxed lunches at cafeteria tables and bond intensely. They buy books and CDs, supporting the publishers who help finance these events. They exchange tips on what works and what doesn't, activities that engage teens and the latest research on adult education. One source of their strength is that they are first friends, who monitor one another's personal sadnesses and successes. They are quick with a casserole, congratulations, or sympathy. No wonder parishioners turn to them so readily during a crisis.

"In media stat virtus," wrote Thomas Aquinas. "In the middle lies the truth." Catechists and DREs (directors of religious education) stand firmly in that middle ground. To most pew folk, they represent the face of the church. Many lay ministers serve as a buffer zone between the people and the hierarchs. If the bishop issues a policy that the altar servers at confirmation must be shorter than he and wear white gloves, it will generate a buzz and some snickers in the professional network, but most ordinary churchgoers will be spared the drama.

How easily these catechists dismiss institutional wackiness. So my mentor, Sister Mary Luke Tobin, SL, once waved aside some bishop's egotism as she would've treated mischievous boys on the playground. How gladly the laity get on with real work, how they hunger for genuine, shaped-in-the-trenches spirituality. Their own quest for meaning is a powerful model for those they instruct. Often, the work on the ground runs years ahead of the concepts or policies about it.

While the effort for professional certification is laudable and continues energetically, these people also deserve blue ribbons for dedicated goodheartedness. They know the science of catechesis (and devote countless summers to learning more). More important, they practice the art, relating to children, teens, and adults with widely different backgrounds, values, and yearnings, shaping them into fragile, ever-changing community. Gently, they guide the human search for meaning and the difficult apprenticeship to Christ.

As a speaker who's only briefly part of each community, I admire from afar their generosity; they dip into their own pockets for supplies, snacks, and educational resources. Gamely, they appreciate or participate themselves in the disconnect between immigrant groups and the dominant culture. They communicate in a variety of languages, but their native tongue is care. Many teachers realize they can't compensate for parental lack of involvement but do their best to make an hour on Tuesday evening the most power-packed experience they can construct.

Children respond like plants in sunlight to authentic teachers who speak in practical, understandable ways. Parents relate well to catechists who are like themselves, approachable because they live with the same realities of puzzling insurance and tax forms, baffling teenagers, dwindling finances, and soaring bills for home repair and health care. Catechists and DREs are more, though; they are models who with those burdens still find time to read in depth, make occasional retreats or days of prayer, minister to needy people, and create sanctuaries in their homes or classrooms.

They don't waste time gnashing their teeth over the gender, sexual orientation, or ethnicity of their coworkers or parishioners. Instead, they compliment Margaret on a dynamite prayer service, invite Marc and his partner to brunch, remind Najeek about PowerPoint class. At the parish level, women denied official validation run the show. Outside the power structure, they're free to be creative, outpacing theological or canonical theories that may someday explain their work.

What is the wellspring of such activity? What is the source of their strength? I can only speculate that they are well grounded. The broad acceptance gained through centering prayer or meditation doesn't dichotomize or polarize. It eschews categories because individuals are so much more interesting and unique. Maybe the official ecumenical movement is stalled in Rome. But Karen from the Lutheran Church shares insights with Episcopal women in a Benedictine parish hall.

Furthermore, these devoted workshop attendees have self-selected; they are clearly committed to learning. When I suggest a new idea or intuition, it's gratifying to see the wave of light wash participants' faces. "I'd never thought of it that way!" they say without a word. In those rare moments dear to a speaker's heart, they articulate an inner shift: "You have no idea how much you've affected me." For such moments it's worth doing time in airport security.

Another subtopic of the workshop genre, growing in popularity, is the women's day of prayer. Meticulously prepared in advance, these events "care for the caregivers." Women flock to a winning combination of sympathetic community, carefully orchestrated details like music and dance, thoughtful gifts, a stimulating speaker, and lovely meals. When I was interviewed by a journalist for the local paper before one of these events, he mused, "and all this energy—all this planning work—done without the diocese!"

Later, I thought about his comment. Such creative independence can be explained by one unruly reality: adults insist on being adults. Eight women with other full-time jobs can in their free time organize an event that draws 320—seventy more people than the conference center holds. They are superbly organized and hospitable; they stretch attendees' imaginations with liturgical dance and new ideas that many in the audience may not have experienced.

Overworked and underpaid, frazzled by dysfunctional relationships, insulted by oppressive hierarchies, and plum tuckered out, catechists and other adults come to workshops to meet a deep need. Galway Kinnell describes it eloquently in his poem "St. Francis and the Sow":

sometimes it is necessary
to reteach a thing its loveliness . . .
retell it in words and touch
it is lovely
until it flowers again from within, of self-blessing.

Joined by prayer and common interests, an intergenerational spectrum comes together, conversation sparkles, and blessings abound. Informally, seasoned catechists counsel newbies. Grandmothers tell young moms to relax—junior probably won't become a serial killer.

The interwoven threads of prayer, learning, and community are a winning combination. So maybe the Catholic people aren't nurtured by the weekly homily or the diocesan newspaper. They search elsewhere and are amply rewarded by innovations that surpass boring language and meaningless abstractions.

Such gatherings have become such a vibrant source of energy. I'll keep coming as long as they'll have me. See you at the airport Friday.

QUESTIONS FOR REFLECTION OR DISCUSSION

- Have you ever attended a gathering such as those described above? What was your response?
- Do you think it happens often that the people within an institution get ahead of the official thinking? Why or why not?

A Catholic Chorus

Rose: A Biblical scholar and teacher, Rose speaks of Catholicism as bred in her bones. Like so many interviewed here, her faith is tied to her family and her ethnic (Irish) background.

"*Ethnicity, poverty, locality and sacrality created the silence, wonder, community, and worshipful atmosphere of the old mass. People didn't complain that it was in a language they didn't understand. They seemed to appreciate its transcendence, an hour set beyond their daily routines. During that time, ordinary concerns didn't vanish; prayers for an alcoholic husband, for a child's success, or a mother's healing bubbled beneath the official surface of 'Dominus vobiscum' or 'Et cum spiritu tuo.'*"

Chapter 18

Why I Study Spanish

Spanish studies began, as many things do, with the Catholic Church. *Digo si, Senor. Oyenos mi Dios. La palabra de Dios.* Yes, Jesus. Hear us, O Lord. The word of the Lord. Most of us can fake a few Spanish songs or mass responses, but I wanted to know more of this lilting language spoken throughout the world. When the gospel is proclaimed bilingually, it's as beautiful as two intertwined vines—but I could only follow one. I was embarrassed when I'd arrive to give a talk, and the organizer would say, "We didn't have enough people for the Spanish track, so we've put them all in your English-speaking one."

Pobrecitos! I could only imagine how cheated I'd feel if I signed up for a workshop in my native language, then had to listen in another. With the help of Dr. Chela Gonzalez, director of religious education for the Archdiocese of Santa Fe, I crafted a halting welcome in Spanish, rehearsed it endlessly, and tried not to insult the audience too much when I bumbled through this opening.

But that wasn't enough. I felt like a dumb *gringa*, neither understanding nor speaking the language of over half the American church. I couldn't even read the Spanish translations of my own books. Twenty-three years of studying French in school hadn't prepared me for the reality of life in the western United States, and increasingly, in other regions.

Drawing even more attention to my incompetence, I had insisted on my children being bilingual. One studied in Guatemala, another in Mexico, and a third learned fluent Spanish (and a few raunchy jokes) working in a hotel kitchen. Whenever I'd get flustered because we were late for a flight or important event, they'd reassure me that we were doing OK: *Estamos bien.*

But this was about more than one small family. There is something compelling about the universality of the Catholic Church. It strikes me every year at the Los Angeles Religious Education Congress, the largest and most diversified gathering of this kind in the country. Asian drummers, African dancers, mariachi musicians, readers and singers from various cultures: all combine their talents for a dramatic opening and eucharistic liturgies that showcase the rich variety within our tradition. "None of us is as smart as all of us" is an axiom that certainly applies to worship. Within a single culture, we can be bland as vanilla pudding. When multiple streams combine, it builds to a crescendo of "Wow."

Furthermore, the bishops of the United States, sensitive to other cultures, have spoken courageously on immigration questions. When the INS raided Swift meat-packing plants, religious leaders pointed to the injustice of separating children from parents whose "crime" was working at jobs most Anglos would reject. While I sympathized mightily, I couldn't express it in a language they would understand. Learning Spanish seemed like a step toward a larger heart.

So every Monday for the last nine months I've trudged to a local campus for Spanish class. My skills are still embarrassing: with limited vocabulary and knowledge of only the present tense, my efforts must seem like a toddler's. What's heartening is the verve of Marianne, our Venezuelan instructor, who must repeat the basics until she wants to shriek. Yet she remains patient and encouraging.

Furthermore, she enhances our study with the *play* of language: the lilt, the nuances, the color and drama. Those who've spoken their native tongue for a long time get complacent with it. We rely on the same, tired expressions repeatedly. In contrast, new brain channels must open and expand as I learn the Spanish for a familiar object or concept. It's fun to see if it parallels English or French, to recognize how colloquialisms reflect the spirit of a people.

Most folks like to be in a place where they feel competent and successful. Yet the other students in this class have moved beyond their comfort zones to risk appearing foolish when they try unfamiliar words or sentence constructions. A small, tentative Pentecost happens in Spanish class, with a similar, powerful wind blowing there.

Another key reason to keep trying is my unofficial coach, Maria, from Mexico. She spends most of the day laundering and folding towels or cleaning at my athletic club. With this job she supports three young sons. Sometimes I'm embarrassed to be taking aerobics class or yoga when she looks exhausted. Yet she remains unfailingly cheerful, greeting all the members in ways that must brighten their dullest days. Her English is limited, but she tries mightily. When I think how hard it must be for her to function in this culture, it makes my struggle to learn *her* language easier.

Maria has graciously taken the role of *mi maestra*, correcting pronunciation, checking homework, and most of all being a cheerleader. "Muy intelligente," she'll crow when I make the slightest attempt. The teacher role seems to transform her; for those twenty minutes she transcends the mountain of towels.

Other drivers listen to music in their cars. My Spanish tapes enthrall with the merry escapades of Carmen and Enrique who'd go to the movies if they could find the pesky *llaves*—keys. The Moreno family enjoys the beach. Perhaps the list of irregular present participles stretches through three long red lights.

Many spiritual writers emphasize the virtues of vulnerability and hesitation. Wandering clueless through a foreign language, we abandon adult precision and are willing to "become like children" again. The hilarity of "beginner's mind" broadcast loud and clear when my overly enthusiastic friend, misunderstanding the pronunciation required by the tilde, wished "Happy Ass" *(ano)* instead of "Happy New Year" *(año)* to armed soldiers in Guatemala City.

When it comes down to it, most of us are motivated by other people. When we do things to gain their approval, improve their lives, strengthen or understand them, we get a glimmer of what the mystical body must be. Not even a paycheck can inspire us like the need of a child, the call of a friend, or the challenge of a relationship. Many years ago Marisol must have planted the seed of my current Spanish study.

She attended a workshop I gave in San Bernardino, California. When the sound technician needed to attach my microphone and I had no pockets, Marisol quickly offered her own belt. What I remember best, though, was not her generosity, not her beauty, but her eyes.

When Marisol described her family, her dark eyes became pools of sadness. Her mother was dying in Guatemala, and she couldn't afford many trips there. It was obvious how close mother and daughter were and how aching their separation must be. I wanted to comfort Marisol in her own language. My lack of Spanish became painful then.

Yet I've carried her image for several years, thinking that a world with Marisol's eyes must be all right. People with such large visions forgive our narrowness. If the human family continues to reach across language gaps and cultural differences, we'll be OK. In unique and different ways, we'll hear, praise, and internalize *la palabra de Dios.*

QUESTIONS FOR REFLECTION OR DISCUSSION

- What in this chapter explains why the Catholic Church generally takes a strong stand on behalf of immigrants?
- Have you ever wanted to be more fluent in another language? If so, describe the circumstances.
- What in this chapter describes the universality of Catholicism?

A Catholic Chorus

Kristen: "My family is far flung, living in different states—my siblings, my mom, my kids. But when I hear the liturgy of the word on Sunday, we're all connected. We're hearing the same Bible stories and relating to them! Sometimes I can't sleep in the middle of the night, or I'm blue during the day. Then I remind myself that somewhere in the world, the mass is happening. Bread and wine is being consecrated into Christ's body and blood. Knowing that buoys me."

Chapter 19

Amazon Warrior

Dorothy Stang

Just when I thought I'd outgrown mentors, a friend introduced me to David Stang. His enthusiasm is contagious for his favorite subject, his sister Dorothy.

"She whacked me around as a kid," he admits. "A tomboy, she played the best football in the family." That tenacity carried her through the Amazon, where she became a feisty defender of the poor and the rainforest. After her death she's still a role model in the arenas of the environment, aging, and women's roles.

Her story has the attributes of heroic legend, so let's tell it that way. First, the setting(s). In Brazil, less than 3 percent of the population owns two-thirds of the arable land. When the government gives land to displaced farm workers, loggers and ranchers burn poor settlements, sell valuable timber, then graze cattle (to supply our McDonald's!). The consequent loss of the rainforest is tragic because it contains 30 percent of the world's biodiversity. Some call it "the lungs of the planet." As it shrinks, global warming increases.

It's hard to imagine a place more distant from Brazil than Dayton, Ohio. Young Dorothy lives here, her backyard a model of organic gardening, where she learns composting and the dangers of pesticides. In 1948, she becomes a Sister of Notre Dame and a teacher. You expect her to become a benevolent nun who dies of old age in a quiet convent, right? That's where her story gets interesting.

Our heroine volunteers for Brazil when her order calls for missionaries. She accompanies families to Para, bordering the rainforest, to defend their land. She asked the right questions there—not minor matters of narrow denominational or territorial concerns, but "How do we preserve the earth's treasures? How do we empower God's beloved people who live upon this land?" Dorothy had the expansive spirit of first-century Roman philosopher Seneca, who declared "The whole world is my own native land."

She organizes people into co-ops, where they learn crop rotation, read the Bible, and worship with music and dance. Because priests are scarce, she becomes the people's "shepherd." As Galatians advises, "There is no longer Jew or Greek, there is no longer slave or free, there is no longer male and female, for all of you are one in Christ Jesus" (3:28). It didn't much matter if she was male or female, ordained or not. What did matter, burningly, was that "no one has greater love than this; to lay down one's life for one's friends" (Jn 15:13).

When her people are attacked, she tells them brusquely, "Quit crying; start rebuilding!" Her old VW Beetle wobbles over bridges with rotting planks—while her passenger David makes a nervous sign of the cross. Dorothy takes the people's case to the government. When officials deny receiving her letters, she burrows through their files till she finds them. Persistently, she asks for protection for poor farmers, but nothing is done.

Amazingly, she keeps this up for thirty-eight *years*. Dorothy starts fruit orchards with women and projects for sustainable development with twelve hundred people. The Brazilian Bar Association names her Humanitarian of the Year in 2004.

Enter the villains. The ranchers hire gunmen who shoot her to death on February 12, 2005. Seeing the gun, Dorothy doesn't run or plead for her life, as most folks would. Fear would've been natural and understandable. Instead, she pulls out her bible and reads the beatitudes aloud. The divine power transcends human limitations; in those final moments, she imitated Christ. She must've spent a lifetime preparing for that climax; now she teaches me how to live.

Breathing a deep lungful of piney mountain air scented with sage, at home in the Rocky Mountains, I recall Dorothy's joy outdoors. Without much institutional church, she found God in the green canopy of trees, the cathedral of forest. Dorothy reminds me that when we lose our sacred connection to the earth, we're stuck with small selves and petty concerns. In film footage she proudly shows off a tree farm, exulting, "We *can* reforest the Amazon."

Dorothy has encouraged me to stop eating beef, since intensive grazing requires destruction of the rainforest. I'm learning "green" alternatives to wasteful habits. Like most North Americans, I have enough stuff and now lean toward a simpler life. David explains, "She was so in love with what she was doing, she didn't notice her dirt floor, primitive plumbing, no electricity." *Holy* once meant pious and passive. But Dorothy models how to "raise Cain" and act for justice. As we baby boomers age, Dorothy is patron saint for slow butterflies and reluctant caterpillars. She didn't remain captive to her traditional upbringing. She probably could've hunkered down into the retirement center, counted her wrinkles, and kept careful tabs on her ailments, as some older folk do. Instead, vivaciously, she tried new things, journeyed to new places. Her face is so youthful it's hard to think of her as seventy-three. If I want to look that luminous at that age, I too must shed fears and take risks.

I want to love as gladly and fully as she did. It's easy to get caught up in trivia: social commitments, work deadlines, domestic chores. But is this how we want to spend the precious coinage of brief lives? At Dorothy's funeral, her friend Sister Jo Anne announced, "We're not going to bury Dorothy; we're going to plant her. Dorothy, *Vive*!" If I want that immortality, I should examine what seeds I'm planting now, how I'll live on in memory.

Dorothy has ruined my easy cop out: How can one small person offset complex and apparently hopeless wrongs? Dorothy and I are the same height, 5'2". Yet look what this giant accomplished: her killers' trials, televised to every Brazilian classroom, have given children hope.

Her family and community won't pursue canonization, preferring to give the poor the money that cause would require. Many already consider Dorothy a saint and martyr. In the early church that's all that mattered. As one biographer said about St. Catherine of Siena, "Someone must've told her women were inferior. She clearly didn't believe it." With regard to women's roles, David has the final word: "Don't *ever* call my sister second class!"

QUESTIONS FOR REFLECTION OR DISCUSSION

- Have you ever had a role model or mentor who enlarged or challenged your life as Dorothy did for the author? Describe this person and the effect.
- Have you ever had a time when you were so in love with what you were doing that you didn't notice aggravations or deprivations? Describe it.

A Catholic Chorus

Lucy: A junior-high teacher and mother of two daughters echoes another speaker's idea, that "religion is about having a relationship with God so we can get some help." She responds: "The best part about being Catholic is the fact that I can rely on prayer to help me through anything. When something comes my way that is challenging, I truly feel like I turn to prayer to have God help me through it. I also love the fact that I can bring my children up with the same morals, values, and dedication to prayer that I have.

"A wonderful example: My Annie (sixth grade) had been sick all weekend, and we had been trying to figure out the issue. Early on Sunday she had horrible stomach pain. As I was googling "appendicitis" on the computer at 5 a.m., she began praying the Rosary through her cries and tears. She had a high fever and was talking funny. Gratefully, her pain was on the left side and not the right, so no appendicitis. After we got her calmed down, gave her a dose of Motrin and got her back to sleep, she slept until noon. When she woke, the first thing she said was, "Mommy, I feel so much better! Prayer solves everything!"

Chapter 20

Singing Mercy

For an hour the women of Empowerment in Denver, Colorado, didn't have to think about their parole officers, unpaid bills, drug tests, applications for housing, or GED studies. As long as they were singing with the Okee Dokee Brothers, they were free, happy, smiling. Women who've made poor choices and been scorned or nudged outside polite society, they simply clap and sing, unworried about past mistakes. While the music plays, they can believe in the promise of "I'll Fly Away" to "a land where joy shall never end."

Who brought about this merciful reprieve—and why? Meet Joe Mailander and Justin Lansing. Childhood friends in Denver, they attended Most Precious Blood Parish School and Regis Jesuit High School together. Then Justin went to Lake Forest College and Joe to St. John's University. During college, they founded a non-profit, The Medicinal Strings, a name that underscores their hope in the healing power of music.

As a bluegrass-folk band with four other performers, their mission is sharing, promoting, and inspiring the arts within the lives of those most in need. That translates to over 120 free concerts since they received non-profit status in 2005. In these, they play for underserved populations of homeless shelters, hospitals, retirement centers, child-care facilities, and soup kitchens.

As a for-profit duo begun after college, Joe and Justin double as The Okee Dokee Brothers, based in Minneapolis. According to their website, their mission is to remind children and adults of their "intrinsic ability to discover, imagine, and create through music." Their original music "reminds audiences of their own make-believes and treehouse-pretendings." The pair performs their own compositions at libraries, schools, bluegrass festivals, and state fairs in Minnesota and Texas. Their newest CD helps English speakers learn Spanish through song.

Mission statements and statistics can be dry, but that's the *last* word to describe this dynamic pair, nicknamed "the kids with beards." Young, funny, and completely unpretentious, they have a knack for inviting the participation of even unlikely musicians. Joe confides: "To be in a church basement with three hundred homeless guys all clapping and stomping: you see how music transforms." Music breaks down barriers between performers and audience, different ethnic groups, age groups, and socio-economic levels.

Sites where both bands have performed agree. Tom Burnham, of Peter & Paul Community Services in St. Louis, described the relentlessness of homelessness: "This population seldom experiences live entertainment of any kind. They're homeless every hour of every day of every week. I've been here more than twenty years, and that absolute expression of joy I saw today at the concert—it's rare."

Justine Zollo of the Gathering Place, a shelter for battered women in Denver, comments: "We give people services all the time. But one of the greatest is to remind them of their humanity in a really positive, beautiful way. That's what I saw in the audience today as the band performed."

A review from CoolMomPicks.com focuses on the concerts for children: "This two-member band from Minneapolis makes twangy, toe-tapping folk music with smart, funny lyrics that are equal parts hillbilly, seven-year-old boy, and your favorite teacher."

How did this all begin? Joe and Justin remember a clear call: Chuck Morris, who books all the top musical acts in Denver, liked their music and wanted to audition them. This was the "Big Time" for college students, and they eagerly agreed to perform the next night. When Joe got home and announced the good news, his mother Rita, director of faith formation at Most Precious Blood Parish, shared the joy. Then she reminded her son: "You're booked at the Broadway Assistance Center tomorrow night."

The band talked and decided the right thing to do was to honor its first commitment. That night at the homeless shelter turned out to be one of the best concerts they'd ever done, and they saw it as their path forward. No regrets about missing their chance at fame; to the women at Empowerment, they're rock stars.

Back to the concert there. Empowerment provides education, employment assistance, health, housing referrals, and support services to women who have endured incarceration, poverty, homelessness, or HIV/AIDS infection. But that wearying list of troubles didn't affect the fun. A tiny air-conditioning unit wedged precariously in a cinder block wall chugged valiantly with minimal effect, but above its rumble, the song soared. Proudly, high and low voices blended for the "wimoweh" chorus of a rousing "Lion Sleeps Tonight." With a rich mix of banjo and guitar, they were off on a roller-coaster ride (with arm swings), then "flying away" and "wading in the water," "down by the riverside."

This concert touched a key theme in the Medicinal Strings/Okee Dokee philosophy: empowering the audience to be players, not passive spectators. "This can't happen without you," they explain at the start. Often in a crisis center, Joe or Justin invites: "You have a song or a story? Want to share it?" And audience members respond, apparently thinking: What have I got to lose with a few gestures, rounds, a call-and-response song, or a tambourine? It would take a steely heart not to be moved by such boyish enthusiasm.

When they ask for volunteers to play instruments during "My Momma Don't 'Low No Music Makin' Here," audience members are eager to participate. A visiting confirmation class joins the regular group, and the unlikely assortment makes music together. Sonya had just served time in prison for meth charges but she shook her maracas—and hips—with glad abandon. Beside her, a candidate for confirmation and the son of a prominent Denver pediatrician played the castanets. Hoisting her tambourine, eighteen-year-old Kelli shook away worries about her three kids. Next in line, a small Asian girl, another confirmation candidate, delicately played her triangle. It was a vibrant reminder of "here comes everybody."

Perhaps it was also church in a broader sense, with God's people a choir larger than ever imagined. It connected with one of the oldest forms of worship, described in Psalm 150: "Give praise with tambourines and dance, praise him with flutes and strings."

Asked the devil's advocate questions—"Will an hour of song really change lives? Create community? Bridge the gap between teenagers whose orthodontia costs more than a client's yearly budget?"—Justin answers thoughtfully, "For them, as for us, awareness grows gradually. Maybe through this experience in eighth grade, a few service projects in high school, travel abroad in college, they'll learn we all have the same emotions."

Though Joe and Justin both shy away from the word *ministry,* they believe community is built through the energy exchange between performers and audience, art and ritual—all experiences "out of ordinary time." Before the concert Justin chatted with a recovering alcoholic in the audience who had said she was having a bad day. But during "Stand by Me" she closed her eyes and remembered her daddy's banjo. An easily accessible blend of Beatles and gospel, Guthrie and gospel, the repertoire stirs dreams of the civil rights movement and memories of simpler childhoods. Some of these songs helped slaves endure a horrific ordeal, or convinced settlers to build one another's barns; their power persists. Maybe the Inuit children of northeastern Alaska should have the final say: "It sure is ice to snow them!"?

So let the reader decide—if this isn't the best of Catholic ministry, what *does* one name their work? Restoring people's dignity, stretching their imaginations, lightening their load—isn't that what Jesus did?

QUESTIONS FOR REFLECTION OR DISCUSSION

- Have you noticed ministries emerging that may not fit the traditional mold, especially among the young?
- Father Greg Boyle, SJ, began Homeboy and Homegirl Industries in Los Angeles to help gang members get jobs and stay out of gangs. One of the services is tattoo removal, which could ultimately save someone's life. Have you ever thought of *that* as a work of mercy? Could it be?

A Catholic Chorus

Margaret: "I feel comfort from votive candles, security from the Rosary. When I can't sleep at night, I hold the beads and draw on the prayers' power, what the Rosary meant to generations before me. It's a way of saying, 'OK, God, you're in control' without a hard thinking or speaking process."

Chapter 21

My Favorite Sister Stories

My long connection with the sisters began in high school, shortly before Vatican II. I was the annoying student who posed the pesky questions that stumped Sr. Harriet, our theology teacher. It didn't take a genius, even in tenth grade, to ask, "If the mass is our most important prayer, why is it in a language we don't understand?" She had more trouble with "Why won't my kindly Baptist relatives go to heaven?" but that may have been my misperception of Catholic teaching. A few years after the Vatican council, Sr. Harriet had the grace to phone. "Remember all those questions?" she laughed. "You were right."

Never once did the Religious of the Sacred Heart tell us that girls should be pretty and dumb. *Au contraire.* They modeled that women should use their gifts and intelligence. One set up our honors program on the same model she'd followed in graduate studies at Oxford University. Department chairs, deans, college presidents? Of course women would fill those roles with skill and dignity.

The sisters adapted with grace and fidelity to enormous changes brought on by the Second Vatican Council, moving out of the cloister and into a society many were unfamiliar with. But they knew, deep down, instinctive human courtesy and compassion. When my mother was dying, her colleagues and friends at the college where she taught were sisters. They walked steadily and courageously through that final illness with us and remained motherly figures to me for years after her death.

Servite Sr. Joyce Rupp, knowing I was trying to write my first book, *Hidden Women of the Gospels*, asked, "How can you concentrate with four kids at home? Use my apartment when I'm away!" I marveled at her understanding and later at her generosity when she wrote the foreword.

Sisters' networks promoted my books and cheered my first efforts at giving retreats. Wait—didn't this work the other way around? Weren't *they* supposed to give retreats to lay people? When a Jesuit director asked Sister Eleanor to give a mother-daughter retreat, she refused. "What would I know about that? Get a mother-daughter team!" Her honesty opened the door for my daughter and me to direct those amazing experiences for five years.

Change didn't flummox such secure women; they were supportive and kind as roles reversed. The Australian Ursulines flew me there to give their province retreat for sisters from South Africa, Thailand, and throughout Australia. I secretly wondered what a frazzled mother of four could possibly tell them, but they were consistently warm and appreciative.

Afterward, the provincial and I spent many hours driving around the country, because they wanted exposure for their speakers in rural areas beyond Sydney. A town west of the Blue Mountains was unusually cool one evening, and most houses don't have central heating. The elderly nun at whose home we were staying sidled up before I began an evening talk. "I've turned on your bed for you," she whispered. I puzzled about that for a while. Turned out she had kindly warmed it up with the "wooly underlay," which we'd call the heated mattress pad.

Back in the United States at a local retreat center, several of us arrived the evening before the retreat began. Sister Rita was somewhat addicted to a harmless television program and asked a Peruvian staff member why none of the TV sets seemed to work. Seeking to reassure her, he grinned broadly, "Yes, we have no channels." That lovely non sequitur quickly upstaged any inspiration I'd hoped to give during the retreat.

The Victory Noll sisters were unwitting stars of the show during the retreat at their motherhouse in Huntington, Indiana. One ninety-three-year-old sister told how she'd visited St. Peter's in Rome on the same day as a mother and her daughter from Kansas. The daughter was wearing shorts, and the guards wouldn't allow her to enter. Her mother was agonizing that they'd come so far and couldn't see any of the treasures within. "Then I remembered," Sister brightened. "I was wearing a half-slip. So right there in the Vatican, I dropped my petticoat. The girl wore it over her shorts; the guards were happy and off they went. They're probably still praying for me."

As I read the elderly sisters the Song of Songs ("Arise, my beloved and come . . . ") some dozed. Others were bent over, their heads poking out like turtles. But they displayed photos of their profession days when, slim and erect, they carried candles and wore bridal gowns. They had taken risks, lived in Bolivia or the adobe buildings of Santa Fe. Now, in walkers or wheelchairs, their tasks are folding napkins worn soft with many uses. Unlikely as it may seem, they are the portrait of fidelity.

On a brilliant spring day at Victory Noll, a spry eighty-nine year old gave a tour of the grounds in her golf cart. She had labeled every tree on the property with a small plaque that identified its species and the name of one of the sisters in their community, living or dead. Some sisters make regular visits to "their" tree. On Arbor Day, fifth graders from the local school visited—and each one left with a sapling to plant at home.

My work in religious education continued my early friendships with the sisters. I remember going to a restaurant for dinner with several sisters after the San Antonio Religious Education Congress. "Watch this," said one in habit as we entered the crowded bar for a drink. "I can clear out this place faster than lightning." Indeed, we were whisked to an empty table in a flash.

One of my best friends, Mary Ann, practices a similar technique. She and I don't like sharing the hotel hot tub with teenagers. So she'll ask kindly if my disease is still contagious, and I'll respond with a sweet inquiry about the state of her (imagined) oozing sores. Funny how fast the kids leave. Meanwhile, I take quiet delight in this Sister of St. Joseph wearing a swimsuit. When I was growing up, nuns were draped in head-to-toe black habits. I'd secretly wondered if they had feet.

The same friend, hearing on the phone that I have a nasty cold, arrives the same day with a basket of citrus. In the same generous way she brought her famous homemade spaghetti to my new home on moving day. She works with the marginalized women of Denver: prostitutes, ex-felons, those who struggle to earn a GED. In her backyard are thirty-seven fruit trees planted by the house's former owner. But where do the birds choose to nest? In a hanging basket on her back porch, where they've hatched many eggs. That speaks volumes about the secure nests she's made for the most frail and vulnerable people.

When, at age nineteen, Mary Ann proposed to her family that it would be fun to become a sister, her dad reacted first: "Oh, just buy her a round-trip ticket. She'll be home from the convent in a week or two." Her brothers chimed in, "Cool—you could be our sister sister!" said Joe. David added, "Sister squared!"

Her dad would have to admit that his only daughter proved him wrong. Many people benefited because she got a one-way ticket—and stayed for over fifty years. The words of the psalmist fit her achievement:

One thing I asked of the Lord,
that will I seek after:
to dwell in the house of the Lord
all the days of my life. (Ps 27:4)

And what a house that has been! Nothing pious or prissy there. A home brimming with laughter, music, flowers, photos of friends and family, handmade curtains and pillows, squirt-gun tournaments, tomatoes, olive oil and garlic, candles, and overflowing life—life spilling into the rose garden and the back porch.

One hallmark of holy people is they're fun to be around. They draw others to themselves because they are so joyful, thoughtful, alive. The true saints aren't dour, law-obsessed people that everyone runs screaming from. They have lots of friends and adventures. They go sky diving and river rafting (although they may not stay in the boat long) and taste all the rich experiences life offers.

Athanasius once said, "The risen Christ makes life a perpetual feast." The only way we can know that feast is through other human beings:

- We know that feast if we've eaten at Mary Ann's table. She can get home from work at 5:30 and have dinner ready by 6—that's some fancy footwork with the loaves and fishes!
- We know that feast if we've had a death in the family—and Mary Ann's zucchini bread is there to comfort us.
- We know that feast when she anticipates our loneliness or sadness and suggests a movie or an outing to feed the soul.
- We know that feast if we've ever heard Mary Ann's talk on gutsy women of the gospel and thought—wow. Maybe the people drawn to Jesus are feisty and fascinating, not dull and distant.
- We know that feast at Empowerment, her work, when a woman deprived of childhood does a perfect spelling paper. Mary Ann gives her a sticker and a big hug and a "Great Job, Babe." Maybe for the first time in her life, that woman knows abundance.

She's given us a glimpse of that face of Jesus who worried more about people being hungry than about how well they kept the Sabbath. Like Mary Ann, he wasn't the least bit bothered by practical realities—what's two hundred days' wages to feed the crowd? The most ancient Christian mosaics show two fish and *four* loaves. Did they get it wrong? No—they were saying that the fifth loaf is each one of us.

My spiritual director, a Sister of Charity in her eighties, fills my annual eight-day retreat with practical guidance. No "consider the lilies of the field" advice from her. She's brutally frank. "You need a financial planner." She had intuited how money worries were undermining my spiritual life—and knew exactly how to improve the situation.

Sister Barb Dreyer, development director for the Sisters of St. Joseph of Carondelet, encourages people not to feel sorry for sisters. Yes, their numbers are fewer, and many no longer wear habits. But those who remain are visible, doing great things. They may be transitioning out of their traditional role as teachers in Catholic schools, but they are discovering other places where they are desperately needed. Lots of people had no idea who nuns were—but became immensely grateful to a sister attorney who negotiated immigration papers, a social worker who found them housing, or an ESL teacher who helped them with English skills for the job market.

Of course, it's impossible to generalize about any group of individuals. Those reporting to the Vatican probably had a hard time summarizing all the varied works and personalities of sisters in the United States. Rigid labels will slide right off: liberal/conservative, outgoing/reserved, active/contemplative. The only generalization that holds true paraphrases John Patrick Shanley's dedication of his play "Doubt." In tribute to the order that taught him in grade school, he says that we've all made fun of sisters and enjoyed jokes at their expense. But few among us have served with more generosity or compassion. *Amen.*

QUESTIONS FOR REFLECTION OR DISCUSSION

- Do you have any favorite sister stories? What are they?
- As the number of vocations to the religious life decreases dramatically, what might the church lose? What might take its place?

A Catholic Chorus

Ari: "I grew up with a Catholic mom and a dad who wasn't, with huge antagonism between them. Maybe as a result, I have lots of questions about religion. That's why I'm so grateful for a Catholic spirituality group where I can speak freely and for people who welcome whatever I say. As Richard Rohr points out, he'd rather be openly confronted about disagreement than receive pious, hypocritical lip service from people who won't voice their differences."

Chapter 22

Catholics in Collaboration

The popular hymn "What Is This Place?" can easily waft beyond church walls. We know that sacred space extends to all creation wherever, quietly and unobtrusively, tender care happens. One site for such compassionate, ecumenical ministry is the Recovery Café in Seattle, Washington. Its black-and-white-striped awnings, big windows, and bright-red door beckon to a welcoming oasis in a neighborhood close to downtown.

What exactly *is* this place? What happens here? To a wide assortment of hurting people, it's a refuge for healing and hope. Alcoholics and addicts further traumatized by homelessness and mental illness are drawn here for beauty, spirituality, community, and transformation.

BLESSED BY BEAUTY

Essential to the café's creed is the power of beauty to restore human dignity and nurture the human spirit. A recent move to a permanent home has increased the space four times, making it possible to hold simultaneous meals, meetings, art classes, counseling, and meditation groups. In a city known for depressing winters, this setting soars with bold color and fresh flowers. Vivid walls painted red, orange, and green echo in the same shades of chairs and coffee mugs. The members' papier-mache sculptures of key words like *forgiveness* hang gracefully on the walls. Bathrooms are immaculate; the space is suffused with light.

At the center of the action lie a coffee bar and a food-service area that rival a posh cafeteria. Healthy vegetables, soups, breads, and fruits abound; depending on the day's donations, restaurant salads and tasty deserts are also on the menu. The place itself brims with the message "your life matters." As founder Killian Noe writes, café visitors "not only hear this message of how loved they are, they see it in the beauty of the space into which they have been welcomed, they taste it in the delicious and nutritious food they are served." Many have never opened a Christmas gift as they receive here or ever made a home in such order and peace.

Executive Director David Coffey (my son) said at the February 11 grand opening of the new center: "This beautiful building is a radical concept in action. It says that no matter the trauma you have suffered, the poor decisions you have made, your zip code or lack of one, what your parents did or didn't do, what addictions or pain you carry, *you are worthy of our best.* This place is not the leftover leftover or the hand me down hand me down. It says to everyone who enters, 'You are welcome; you are my brother, my sister, my daughter, my son.'"

Similar services to at-risk populations may be provided elsewhere in dreary gray rooms with cinder-block walls. But grimness would contradict the core belief of the café: when you are connected to some small measure of the world's suffering, you are also connected to all the world's hope. That is a connection to celebrate with banners, music, beauty.

GROUNDED IN SPIRITUALITY

A guiding principle in this community's philosophy is that those who claim to take Jesus seriously must also take the poor and excluded seriously. If God is utterly "other," then we must encounter God in those most unlike ourselves. Those who have been sheltered and privileged may be startled when Recovery Café members are interviewed about the highlights of their childhoods. Sabrina reaches far back into memory, then smiles, "When I was nine, I got a store-bought dress." Gavin remembers forty years later, "My dad hugged me . . . once."

Killian Noe, named Distinguished Alumni by Yale Divinity School, has an uncanny ability to facilitate a meeting with donors, then cross the hall and, ten minutes later, give total empathy to people scarred by abuse, mental illness, and addictions. The source of her strength is a commitment to daily centering prayer, which she teaches members through the school for recovery.

Each day at the café begins with a half hour of silent prayer. Merton and Keating would be proud to see people who have been abused, defeated, and dismissed by society recognizing that only God can heal their deep wounds. When the surface is chaotic, they turn to the core of their being and pass into God's heart. With utmost courtesy God transforms layers of scar tissue to unfold God's dream for each individual.

HEALED BY COMMUNITY

"We have never seen anyone who tried to make it on his or her own stay clean," writes Noe in her book *Finding Our Way Home: Addictions and Divine Love*. An authentic community, where individuals are known and loved, is central to reclaiming a life from addiction. Members belong to others who will hold them accountable for "who we say we want to become." They have *reason* to show up, since genuine relationships are the only ways to change entrenched habits.

The activities of an ordinary day here prove the Zen proverb: There are some things that can be known only by rubbing two people together. Christians have long believed that the flesh is the only place where we can meet God. The body, scarred or bent, wounded or wrinkled as it may be, is the site of incarnation. Café members honor one another, sometimes even before they are able to honor themselves.

So the physical, no matter how disheveled or unraveled its appearance may seem, is reverenced here. People in recovery can understand a God who insists on acting distressingly unlike God. Jesus endured the kinds of shame, humiliation, and scorn from both church and state authorities that they know so well. Café members are well equipped to understand Graham Greene's idea, "You can't conceive . . . nor can I or anyone, the appalling strangeness of the mercy of God."

At a recovery circle, women with mental-health challenges, including addiction, discuss the dilemma: If one brick is suddenly pulled from a wall, what prevents it from collapsing? The leader's analogy: If we remove one destructive behavior, what do we put in its place? Many sympathized when a member admitted, "I miss my heroin high." Sally, a recovery veteran of six years, quietly names her "replacement": "service without any expectation of the outcome." How many who have devoutly practiced spirituality in more protected circumstances can "let go" that trustingly?

Support pours from other women. When one needs to be in denial, the others allow it for a while, until she's able to stare down the harsh truths they've all faced. As a newcomer recounts her career with the Beijing ballet, others don't question; they simply affirm and encourage. When one expresses fear about a court date or another announces her cancer has returned, the others murmur sympathetically, "We'll pray you through it."

A constant refrain is "We're so glad you came." Other members who have "hit bottom" know how hard it is to drag oneself to yet another support group or Twelve-Step meeting. No one can imagine the tragedies that have brought people here, the cruelties that have damaged the inner child so beloved to God. We who find it hard to let go of past mistakes could learn from those who've turned that into an art form.

Since everyone at the café is seeking to stay in recovery from mental-health challenges/addictions, isolation puts them at risk. So, abundant activities are sandwiched between a healthy lunch and dinner: classes in meditation, knitting, yoga, art; meetings for Alcoholics Anonymous, Narcotics Anonymous, Gamblers Anonymous, Al-Anon, and Overeaters Anonymous; clubs for running and walking; referrals to other helping hands. The only requirement for these free services sounds touchingly realistic: must be sober for today.

In her youth Abigail frequented the bars in the café's neighborhood. She explained that she once tried to drink away the sorrow of never having "the M-R-S. and the white picket fence." Now in her eighties and a staunch member, she decks herself in bows, ruffles, and blouses to match the season. The grand opening calls for special dress-up clothes. In an unspoken tribute to the inclusivity of the place, Abigail ignores the "reserved" signs in the front row for major donors and seats herself next to the representative for the Gates Foundation. Right where she belongs.

In an energetic interfaith dynamic, such a beautiful, lively place attracts more generosity and the community expands. One parish cooks Thanksgiving dinner; another provides weekly flowers. Starbucks donates a latte machine; Top Pot bakery sends a generous, steady supply of doughnuts. Homeless and home blessed join together in a rare synchronicity. All know they are human, hungry, and weak in different ways.

One art project is symbolic of the creative work done here. Local artists volunteer to teach café members to create glass mosaic panels. Part of the project includes field trips to the Tacoma Museum of Glass and a glass studio. One participant expressed her gratitude: "Thank you for helping us make whole again what was once shattered."

Statistics can be mind numbing: 13,500 meals served in a year, more than 570 recovery circles a year. More touching are the volunteers who consistently donate homemade birthday cakes for members' milestones: "belly button" birthdays and anniversaries of sobriety.

TRANSFORMED BY GOD'S DREAM

Engraved on the breath and bone of this community is Richard Rohr's axiom: Pain that is not transformed is transmitted. The café understands this change in a way that sounds Ignatian: it wants all persons to realize God's dream for them, knowing they are loved and becoming an instrument of that love to others. While many of us have heard that message in clean, quiet retreat centers, it takes on raw urgency for people living perilously under tarps or bridges. It's easy to quit before the miracle happens.

A former alcoholic who now donates his time to helping others in the same situation said, "All those years I lost as a husband and father—those years are gone, and there is no way to get them back. All I can do is try to help someone who is traveling the road I was on so that he won't have to wake up one day and discover his son grew up while he was getting high."

The proof of the pudding lies in dramatically changed lives. Nine out of ten Recovery Café members suffered some significant childhood trauma.

Drug and alcohol use was one way to self-medicate their pain. For instance, one member had all his ribs broken at the age of thirteen by a foster parent. Another winces as he recalls his sister covered with black-and-blue marks from an abusive stepfather.

Members name and grieve those traumas. Then from the ashes can come flickers of hope and remarkable successes: A former prostitute becomes a responsible mom, student, then nurse. A girl who watched her mother kill her abusive father celebrates two years heroin-free. A gang member relinquishes his gun.

Sometimes that flame of divine light is smothered; some die chained to their addictions. But others continue to wrestle with the question, "Do we really believe that God is creative enough to take all that's happened to us and use it in shaping the person we were created to become?" An incest survivor explains that love had once come at such a high cost, she wanted no part of it. Meeting unconditional love here for the first time began her healing. Many who've been told they were worthless delight in learning they are worth something.

While there is no financial charge to members for café services, the personal cost can be grueling: overcoming childhood abuse, low self-esteem, and long-established patterns of addiction. Those who rely on Twelve-Step meetings can attend twenty-two a week here. Wisely, the staff avoids inventing the wheel and utilizes a proven method that works as one part of its innovative program.

Once a month "Open Mic" night gives people who have never spoken in public a chance to sing, read their poetry, tell their stories. Rick, a member who has published his poems in the café's collection, wrote of the grand opening:

New classrooms, new offices.
The same transforming support.
New location, new space.
The same care.
New period of growth.
The same old Recovery Café.

A coffee shop perches on almost every corner in Seattle. What if each intersection in every city had a center for healing and hope similar to the café? Some believe that the liturgy of the church should then become the liturgy of the neighbor. From that standpoint, Recovery Café is a cathedral.[1]

[1] For more information, see www.recoverycafe.org.

QUESTIONS FOR REFLECTION OR DISCUSSION

- In your area, is there a place similar to Recovery Café where the works of mercy are practiced daily?
- What do you think is meant by the phrase in Ignatian spirituality, "weak enough to carry God's dream"?

A Catholic Chorus

Sam: "The faith offers us a healthy way to approach death. The ritual comforts people by saying, 'It's not the end; we'll see this person again.' The death is still sad, but the power of ritual helps us say goodbye—for a while. I'm also impressed by a vast social services network that lives out the beatitudes."

Chapter 23

The Gospel according to Luke

Sometimes a person epitomizes the best of being Catholic, giving the idea a unique personal flavor. Several characters who do so are profiled in this section, but Sister Mary Luke Tobin had a dramatic influence on many and was a personal mentor to me.

A dancer as a girl, she continued to dance into her nineties before the altar like David before the ark. Always inquisitive, she was a voracious reader and energetic explorer throughout a long life. A member of the Sisters of Loretto, she served as their president for twelve years. When elected to the presidency of the Leadership Conference of Women Religious at the time that Vatican II was starting, she decided to see what was up. Halfway across the Atlantic, a call came in: she'd been *invited* to attend, even though she planned to crash the party anyway. She was the only American among the few women invited and was one of three who participated in drafting documents.

During "discussions" with a conservative cardinal there, she advocated for women religious to wear less restrictive garb than the full habits common before the sixties. He would revise her initial sketches so a sleeve touched the wrist or a skirt, the floor. As a relationship with some tension drew to an end, they told each other goodbye. "Sister, I want you to know that everything I've done, I've done because I love the church," he said. "Ah, Cardinal: everything I've done, I've done because I love the church!" she replied. Lovers of the church can span a wide spectrum.

Long an advocate for peace and justice, she was jailed several times for protests against the Vietnam war and subsequent wars. (At one point, realizing it would take a long time to process all who were under arrest, Luke organized them into a big circle and taught them Sufi dances. The guards seemed baffled, but amused.) She was also a close friend of Trappist author Thomas Merton, who lived near her motherhouse in Nerinx, Kentucky.

Her relevance to the question of "what's best in the church" is best illustrated in a story. Maureen McCormick, SL, tells of making an eight-day retreat before she took final vows as a Sister of Loretto. It was a big event, and excitement was high as she gathered with her class. In those days only priests gave retreats—and the one giving theirs was "colossally disappointing." Because it was a silent retreat (a Catholic phenomenon still found in some places today), participants couldn't even compare notes on particularly horrifying nuggets.

When the eight dreadful days finally croaked to an end, the young sisters gathered with an older leader, Sr. Mary Luke Tobin. Before anyone could complain, she plunged in. "What did you like best about the retreat?" she asked, setting the tone. Amazingly, everyone found something positive to praise, though it was probably an imaginative stretch. No fool, Luke knew the retreat had been a disaster. But her question is the same one that underlies this book. Sure, there's widespread depression in churchland, and formidable negatives abound. But what do we like *best*?

On the day Pope John Paul II was beatified at the Vatican, another group gathered in Denver to honor this formidable woman. It was a different crowd than Rome's, an audience that had the particular spirit of Vatican II fans. They'd endured the church of the 1950s and knew firsthand its narrow rigidity. They'd never grow nostalgic about the glories of the church before the council, when everyone knew his or her "place" in the pecking order, and every question had a ready-made, one-size-fits-all, black-and-white answer (probably found in the *Baltimore Catechism*). They'd been invigorated by the sense of openness the council brought and the changes it had initiated. They were disheartened by the way recent pontiffs and bishops had begun to dismantle its far-sighted teachings.

It's hard to appreciate virtues in the abstract. But Luke gave them flesh in a direct, almost brusque, completely human way. Some which shone from her most clearly appeared in the stories that day, and in an interview with her at age eighty-one.

HOPE

At the seminar honoring Luke, panelist Father Martin Lally, speaking about the depression many feel about the Catholic Church, thought he could predict accurately how Luke would respond. "She'd look for the points of hope," he said, "and she'd find them in this room." His listeners, understanding his discouragement, laughed and clapped their approval, appreciated his validation.

A life-long learner, Luke had grown up in a home that valued the arts, and Thursday was the highlight of the week. That was Library Day and meant bringing home a big stack of new books. This attitude carried over into her study as a religious, exploring the writings of new theologians and poets, inviting leading thinkers to address her students.

She'd see people filling in the chapters beneath the headings Jesus gave in the gospel. "The marvelous reality of God's continual presence to every one of us, within every one of us, could accompany us throughout our days, could be the form of our prayer, and could be the basis of our action," she'd said.

VIBRANT SPIRITUALITY

Luke saw prayer and action as closely integrated. "Prayer that doesn't flow into action is empty, to say the least. Action without prayer will soon thin out."

She called prayer "a simple living in God's presence, without a lot of words or thoughts. In other words, the prayer becomes a reflection on one's true center, one's true nature." By centering on God's presence within, Luke was "making an act of faith, saying I truly believe God is present in me and with me." Our prayer becomes our response to God's presence within everyone else.

Making that reality truly living and vivid is an effort which didn't deter Luke. "We have everything we need to make that happen. In other words, find the gifts you have within you, including the God who is already present there." We may not really believe we have such resources and don't even have to earn these gifts. So we have trouble trusting God, and we lack confidence.

Luke gave as an example having a confrontation—which no one likes to do. Prayer was her preparation, carrying out the yes said earlier to God. If she faced, for example, a hostile official about environmental pollution or migrant workers' housing, she would remember that "this official—being human—has this marvelous capacity to be more than what he is, to discover what he has, God's presence within him, and to respond to that. . . . When I am talking to him I trust in that reality."

REVERENCE FOR THE PERSON

At the heart of Luke's respect, even for her adversaries, was a Karl Rahner saying she passed out on cards to countless people, and quoted in all her talks: "Every single human being is an event of the absolute, radical, free self-communication of God." According to that, Luke says, "God is forever and always communicating God's self to me in a way that is free and liberating and unmerited and forgiving."

Perhaps because of that belief, Luke was notably engaged with other traditions—a walking ecumenical movement long before the term was coined. She could find God's tremendous realities everywhere, a light that must have brightened her life journey. Never restricted by "churchiness," she consequently strode ahead of her time, outside narrow boxes.

Luke regretted that people were "tied down by so many strings that we do not do what we really want to do, which, at the same time, is what God wants us to do." Yet, she believed "that the great goodness in people is real. It just doesn't get a chance to surface. It's blocked out and pushed down by so much. The capacity we have for the divine is so real and so great but we have it covered with all kinds of irrelevant things and, as a result, we don't even know we have it."

At eighty-one she was growing more relaxed about her faults. "I expect to be touchy and cantankerous on occasions, but I don't think it's as important to God as I once did."

PRACTICALITY

When a young sister unthinkingly pulled out a cigarette in that holy of holies, the motherhouse, Luke didn't bat an eye. She simply leaned over and lit it. She'd probably learned the wisdom of "pick your battles," and this wasn't an issue worth debating with a sister so deeply immersed in social justice that she founded, lived, and breathed the Catholic Worker soup kitchen in Denver.

A minister who went to Luke for spiritual direction agonized over the fact that during a particularly difficult patch, she couldn't meditate or pray. "I should be able to do that always, shouldn't I?" she fretted. "Bah!" retorted Luke. "At this stage, you focus on putting one foot in front of the other, then when you're through the crisis, *that's* the time to reflect back on it."

Luke suggested following the Buddhist practice of ringing a little bell regularly to call ourselves to the truest place within, where God resides. But she realized that forms of the bell, such as an inspiring quote, a statue, or a flower could quickly become stale. For that reason, "we must continually refresh our reminders."

She could have been pious or peachy, conforming more closely to the "nunny" mold of her era. Instead, Luke forged beyond stereotypes and created a new definition for *best.*[1]

---

[1] The quotations in this chapter are drawn from "Prayer and Action, Action and Prayer: An Interview with Mary Luke Tobin by Kathy Coffey," *Praying Magazine* (March-April 1990), 18–23.

QUESTIONS FOR REFLECTION OR DISCUSSION

- *What strikes you most about Sister Mary Luke Tobin?*
- *If you sat down with Luke for a cup of tea, what would you like to ask her? How do you think she'd respond?*
- *Who do you think should receive the "Best of Being Catholic" award? Describe this person (living or dead).*

A Catholic Chorus

Alissa: A realtor in her sixties recalls "as if yesterday" the moment when, at age fourteen, she knew with lightning clarity that her grandma wouldn't go to hell for marrying an Episcopalian and leaving the Catholic Church. (At that time, some were taught the "no salvation outside the Catholic Church" error. Others attribute this widespread misconception to children over-dramatizing a more subtly nuanced belief.) In high school she learned the term for her surety: an informed conscience. "It's a stunning reversal of dependence on priests or bishops to take responsibility for our key personal decisions. Of course, we get good advice and consider the church's centuries-old wisdom. But this principle honors the individual's ability to research a vexing question, reflect on it, then act in total confidence that our essential natural goodness can't wander too far astray."

Megan: At her sixty-fourth birthday party, Megan answers without hesitation. Her favorite part of being Catholic is the writers. By profession a nurse, she's a passionate reader with interests in theology and politics. Books fill her home; she subscribes to many periodicals. Favorite authors have modeled respectful ways to disagree with "official" teaching and present thoughtful, valid insights that may run counter to institutional publications.

Megan remembers a turning point in her spiritual life when she was forty-one. A sensitive priest, instead of imposing rules, asked, "You're bright, Megan. What do you think?"

Alissa and Megan agree that they like the ability to say, "I don't care about the hierarchy. I live a perfectly good Catholic life with almost no reference to the Vatican or the U.S. Council of Catholic Bishops. I can shape my essential beliefs with confidence in my own ability to choose."

Chapter 24

A Smorgasbord of Spirituality Styles

"What's your spirituality style?" Upon first hearing this question, we might think it too hip and folksy. We'd harrumph, "My faith isn't like designer jeans or the newest iPhone!"

But now that we've been introduced to various personality types through psychological tests, and to many different learning styles, it makes sense to have varying spirituality style as well. Individuals are distinct in the ways we process information or relate to others and the world, so we must also be unique in that intimate arena of spirituality.

For example, Alejandra found centering prayer a real source of nourishment and serenity in busy days as a mother and grandmother. After months of telling her husband how wonderful it was, she finally persuaded him to join her for a session. He was twitchy and uncomfortable, amazed that people would sit for a long time without speaking. The ultimate puzzle came as they left, when Alejandra made a donation. *"What?"* he sputtered. *"You paid money to sit in silence*?" Clearly, the two had different spirituality styles.

Fortunately the Catholic tradition offers as many styles as a richly stocked smorgasbord. "You don't like roast beef? Then try the chicken" seems like obvious advice at a restaurant. So why do we stay with prayer forms that fail to nourish and repeat processes that don't deliver? Fortunately, there is no *One Right Way.* We're blessed to have an abundance of different approaches and the freedom to choose what suits best. Just as biodiversity strengthens a forest or field, so Christians are enriched by an abundance of spirituality styles.

The descriptions that follow are necessarily brief, and the selection of styles somewhat arbitrary. But the hope is that the reader will resonate with one or more and eventually try more than this first taste. All spirituality styles are meant to bring us to the same ends: growing closer to God and loving others better. So the genuine measure of a style is whether it accomplishes this for us.

Benedictine Sister Joan Chittister defines spirituality as "the way we express a living faith in a real world . . . the sum total of the attitudes and actions that define our life of faith."[1] Over the centuries it's been defined many ways, beginning with martyrdom and self-denial, evolving toward pious practices, especially for priests and nuns. Vatican II's "call to universal holiness" awakened us to the value of lay people practicing their spirituality outside the cloister, out in a world that desperately needs it. We began to see that a mom calming a fussy two-year-old is just as spiritual as a monk saying the Divine Office. The way we live and pray is thus the voice or expression of a deeply held commitment.

BENEDICTINE—REVERENCE FOR THE ORDINARY

While some classical names for spiritual styles originated with different religious orders, they have evolved into forms that fit the laity. Many are now discovering that anything which has flourished since the sixth century deserves serious consideration. Written by a lay person for lay people, the Benedictine *Rule* gives a special lens on the ordinary, affirming that God is found there.

Benedictine Sister Joan Chittister describes a style she's followed most of her adult life that "simply takes the dust and clay of every day and turns it into beauty."[2] St. Benedict was concerned not so much with mysticism or denial as with how to make "here and now right and holy."[3] For that reason, Benedictines see the tools they use daily—spatula, shovel, or computer—as being as sacred as the altar vessels. Father Thomas Berry explains this stance: "reverence will be total, or it will not be at all."[4]

The architecture of medieval monasteries such as Canterbury reflect a life balanced among prayer, study, and work. The spiritual self is nurtured in the church, the physical in dormitory and dining room, and the mind in the library. When our lives seem out of whack, we should see if one part has ballooned out of balance. Are we getting adequate sleep and healthy nutrition? Does overwork dominate our days?

Most important, the central core of the monastery was open space. The cloisters enclosed a garden, open to the sky, in which a fountain or well stood. Author Esther De Waal describes "the audacity of a way of life that put uncluttered space, emptiness, at its heart." She points out that we, too, must keep an inner place free and open, watered, and refreshed by God.[5]

---

[1] *Wisdom Distilled from the Daily* (New York: HarperCollins, 1991), 4–5.

[2] Ibid., 7.

[3] Ibid., 6.

[4] *The Dream of the Earth* (San Francisco: Sierra Club Books, 1988).

[5] *Lost in Wonder* (Collegeville, MN: Liturgical Press, 2003), 10.

Given the chaos of contemporary life, this spirituality is firmly grounded in four anchors: the *Rule,* the gospel, the wisdom of the community, and the particular circumstances of a person's life. It is both steadying and flexible. Prayer is a regular part of the rhythm of each day—not only when it's convenient or comfortable—because praising God is why we're here.

Those drawn to this style know that some things can be learned only in community or family. The social dimension of life corrects our craziness and helps us mature. People who have gone through crisis or tragedy attest that God is present through the kind eyes and tender touches of other people.

The preferred form of prayer for this style is liturgy, psalms, or hymns sung together. Transcending our unique styles, one sentence from the *Rule* speaks to all, sounding clear as a bell on a frosty morning: "Let them prefer nothing whatever to Christ" (72:11).

CARMELITE—DEPTHS OF SILENCE

While it may seem contradictory, placing community and solitude together here shows that the roomy house of Christian spirituality isn't a simplistic either/or but a place for both/and. We need solos *and* we need a full chorus. The tradition has always emphasized the value of silence, entering into the stillness of our hearts to find God. If we fear silence, we risk becoming shallow or fickle, never quite sure what we believe or who we are.

The prayer of Trappist Thomas Merton perfectly expresses this style: "To be here with the silence of Sonship in my heart is to be a center in which all things converge upon you. . . . Therefore, Father, I beg you to keep me in this silence so that I may learn from it the word of your peace and the word of your mercy and the word of your gentleness to the world: and that through me perhaps your word of peace may make itself heard where it has not been possible for anyone to hear it for a long time."[6]

Note that we don't enter silence to escape the world but to embrace it better. We listen long and hard for God's word in order to get it right when we speak to others. In a noisy world, with chatter, traffic, and the constant blare of TV, radio, and iPods, silence is the necessary antidote in order to remember what matters. As Meister Eckhart wrote, "Nothing so much approximates the language of God as silence."

People who make an annual silent retreat or practice centering prayer may not know exactly what happens there. But they leave the silence refreshed, more aware that they dwell within God's prodigious love, more conscious of how to serve others.

---

[6] *Conjectures of a Guilty Bystander* (Garden City, NY: Image, 1968), 178.

EASTERN TRADITIONS

The human longing for the divine is found in all cultures. Some say that current interest in Eastern religions springs from a disaffection with Western forms, especially their tendencies toward domination, sexism, and exclusion. A more positive stance identifies *Jesus* as an Eastern thinker and encourages explorations that enhance the richness of Christianity. The world's different belief systems follow parallel tracks.

While the subject is far too broad to treat adequately in a short space, let's touch on three contemporary examples of this approach. The first is the worldwide admiration for the Dalai Lama, who escaped his native Tibet when the Chinese invaded it. Despite his exile and the oppression of his people, he has remained resolutely peaceful, a commitment for which he won the Nobel Prize in 1989.

His travels have introduced many to the essentials of Buddhism, such as that wisdom—the ability to see things rightly—becomes compassion. His books are a source for additional learning.

From Thich Nhat Hanh, many learn attention to the present moment. Whether washing the dishes or eating an orange, we focus on the *now*, not worrying about past or future. Even our negative emotions, he teaches, should be welcomed, cradling anger as we'd rock a crying baby.

Over a million people annually are starting yoga, a moving meditation. They find that reverencing the body, stretching it, and resting it appropriately relieve stress and alleviate pain. They also rediscover the importance of breath, stressed by all religious traditions, but often forgotten in packed schedules. When we are tense, we resort to rapid, shallow breathing. Instead, we need the long deep breath, drawing in energy, releasing negativity. They learn "beginner's mind," or what Jesus called becoming like little children. Finally, they appreciate the absence of competition, the uniqueness of each person, and new movements for the body opening new channels for the brain.

FRANCISCAN—CREATION

Sam may not join the Franciscans, but he feels closest to God when he's working in his garden, weeding the tomatoes, and admiring the light on their leaves. He's interested in the early roots of this style, expressed in St. Francis's "Canticle of the Sun." Beauty is his door to the sacred. He likes the contemporary version, creation spirituality, reading books by Thomas Barry or Wendell Berry, the new cosmology presented in a number of books, including those of Jim Conlon, or the poetry of Mary Oliver, which praises nature and finds there the inspiration for living well.

"To a Franciscan, the whole world is a tabernacle." People who draw energy and inspiration from God's creation naturally want to preserve it. Their spirituality might find expression in recycling, organic gardening, working for cleaner air and water, preserving the rainforest, or dedication to other environmental issues. Sitting quietly beside a stream reminds them of the flow of God's life, the abundance of God's care, the essence of God's nature, which is infinitely creative.

IGNATIAN—STAND FOR JUSTICE

Ignatian spirituality is best summarized by the motto "finding God in all things." One of the finest contemporary interpreters of this style is William Barry, SJ.

St. Ignatius believed our deep desires are healthy, leading us toward the God who made us. While this may seem mysterious, we ultimately long for union with God. The founder of the Jesuits encouraged people to develop an intimate relationship with a God who isn't punitive, tyrannical, or obsessed with rules. Instead, this God desires what is best for us, and God's creative actions bring it about. Our task is to align our desires with God's. We discern the path for which we were created by noting whether we feel empowered and joyful about a decision or depressed and drained by it.

In this style we look at the texts of our lives to see where God is active. We savor what Ignatius called the "consolations," seeing what has brought us peace and joy so we can repeat those experiences. We also look at the "desolations," which make us angry or miserable, with an intention of avoiding those situations. Over time, we establish a pattern of seeking what is life giving, staying away from the pitfalls that distract from God's peace.

SOLIDARITY

We stand with one another because God first stood with us. Symbolically, this incarnation is represented in the mingling of water and wine during the eucharistic liturgy. "By the mystery of this water and wine, may we come to share in the divinity of Christ who humbled himself to share in our humanity," we pray. The only way the Jewish and Christian people have known God is as part of the struggle. The Bible shows God active in storms and upheavals, crises and battle, tragedy and division. In the Hebrew scriptures the priestly work of intercession meant identifying with the people's suffering.

After the Spanish conquest the Mexican people were devastated. They had nothing left and harbored a collective death wish. When Mary appeared ten years later *as one of them,* a native woman at Guadalupe, she restored their will to live. If God stands with us, and we stand together, we have less to fear than we do as shaky individuals.

A spirituality that tries to isolate itself from the world's sorrows is doomed to fail. In fact, as Kenneth Leech points out, "The word private comes from the Latin *privatio*, which means robbery. To the Christian, nothing is private, least of all prayer. . . . That is the meaning of the symbol of the Trinity: that in God there is social life, community, sharing."[7]

This may not translate to gigantic deeds but to simple practices such as turning off the TV, listening instead to a child's rambling story, answering the phone even when caller ID signals an annoying acquaintance, sending a card or email to one who's grieving. At a national level it's writing to members of Congress to ensure children's health insurance, or participating in the growing movement to close the School of the Americas, renamed the Western Hemisphere Institute for Security Cooperation. Christians in Latin America have given us not only the name for the struggle, *la lucha*, but also the image; together, we can more effectively fight injustice and bring about God's kingdom than we can alone.

THOMISTIC—INTELLECTUAL VIGOR

Some like a logical, carefully reasoned, thoughtful approach to faith. They enjoy brilliant works like Thomas Aquinas's *Summa Theologica* or Teresa of Avila's *Interior Castle.* They don't respond eagerly to guided meditation or liturgical dance; they have a passion for truth and order.

A form of prayer that often appeals to these thinkers is the *lectio divina*, with its orderly four steps: slowly reading a scripture passage, meditating on God's message within it, praying over it, and contemplating its meaning.

Thinkers like an approach that's *not* "touchy feely." Scholars at universities can present the orderly structure of Christian belief without embarrassment. It contains elegant proofs for God's existence and moral behavior, fascinating background on scripture, enough thought-provoking material to engage a seeker throughout a lifetime.

The dimension of learning seems sadly neglected when people proclaim, "We've always done it this way." "Not exactly," the scholar responds. "The practice of confirmation changed dramatically in the ninth century, as did clerical celibacy in the eleventh." Studying church history gives a sense of where we've been and how that affects where we're going.

Some spiritual directors say that the only way we can fail at prayer is by not showing up. Surveying many spirituality styles, we can appreciate the

---

7 *True Prayer* (Harrisburg, PA: Morehouse Publishing, 1985).

healthy variety of a smorgasbord that nurtures at the deepest level. As the Italians say, *mange bene,* come and eat—well.

QUESTIONS FOR REFLECTION OR DISCUSSION

- To which style—or combination of styles—are you most attracted? Why?
- How has the church benefited from such a broad variety of styles?

A Catholic Chorus

Ben: A theologian, husband, dad, author, and editor answers, "The best thing about the church is Jesus, the most free person who ever lived. He lived in a situation like ours, with authorities he hadn't put in place defining how he should live every minuscule detail of daily life, read scripture, and worship. He wouldn't agree, and he wouldn't act as they dictated. Instead, he wanted a community of care and compassion, which the church has offered for centuries. The reason the abuse scandal is so cancerous is that it eats at the very heart of what the church should be.

"When Jesus raised the question, 'How does one live in relation to God?' everyone had an opinion. Since Jesus refused to accept other people's ideas, it was simply a matter of time until they kicked him out. He had many issues with religious authorities of his day; our issues are similar. Within two generations after Jesus the church had established a comfy patriarchy. It quickly imported the cultural customs of its day rather than follow the counter-cultural direction of Jesus."

Ben also points to the fact that hundreds of years before governments devised a "safety net," Catholics were starting soup kitchens, hospitals, and orphanages. Cathedral schools have a long history, preceding even regular schools. In a long educational tradition many people gave their lives to teaching: sisters, priests, brothers, laity.

In the early days of Christianity, medical care was poor. Often the seriously ill were simply left to die. But Christians introduced a new approach, one that hardly seems novel today. Instead of neglecting the sick, they cared for them, providing water and food, doing what they could to ease the suffering. Perhaps as an unintended bonus, this practice contributed to Christian longevity. While plagues wiped out huge populations, the numbers of Christians rose steadily.

Rodney Stark, a Texas sociologist, explored this phenomenon in The Rise of Christianity. *He pointed to the care of the sick as explaining why 50 to 120 followers at Pentecost could become the dominant section of the Roman Empire, with one million members, in less than three centuries.*

The long tradition and broad spread of Catholicism appeals to many. "I like a connection with Christ that's over two thousand years old. This deep rooting in history has both good and bad sides. But somehow, it makes me skeptical of 'The Church for What's Happening Now.'"

One of the best things the Catholic Church ever did was encourage people to seek God in new ways. The channel from the individual to God was direct; it didn't flow only through the ordained. Therefore, everyone is equidistant from the Holy Spirit. This led to many seekers establishing religious orders, each one a unique effort to live as an embodiment of God's kingdom.

What we have in the church is more important than priests and bishops. Ben cites the doctrine of ex opere operato, *that is, that the grace of the sacrament doesn't depend on the priest or minister. Even if he's a pedophile, the sacrament remains a valid channel.*

A great good resides in the people. If we could see them as they really are—filled with God's life, the divinity within sometimes flashing out—we'd never treat them the same. All humanity is involved in the process of transfiguration, moving to the point where God's life takes over in us. Then we can say with Paul, "It is no longer I who live, but it is Christ who lives in me" (Gal 2:20).

Jesus treated everyone with utter respect, care, and compassion. He always gave them their dignity and drew them one step closer to God. The most free person we know, Jesus refused to get caught in reductionism or abstraction, like the law. Instead, he posed questions like, "What about this woman?" redirecting the conversation to the concrete individual.

About the Author

Kathy Coffey was especially energized by the interviews she did for *The Best of Being Catholic*, and the variety of responses to the question, "What's best?" Author of many award-winning books like *Hidden Women of the Gospels, God in the Moment: Making Every Day a Prayer*, and *Women of Mercy*, she is available to give workshops or retreats on the topics of her books, and other catechetical presentations. Kathy has spoken at many national, international and diocesan gatherings. The mother of four and grandmother of two, she lives in Denver, Colorado. For more information, see her website: kathyjcoffey.wordpress.com.

Permissions/Credits

Chapter 8 first appeared as "Being Catholic Means Finding God at Every Turn" in the *National Catholic Reporter* (NCRonline.org), July 31, 2010.

An earlier version of Chapter 9 was originally published as "A Rite to Remember," in *U.S. Catholic* magazine. Reprinted by permission of *U.S. Catholic* magazine (uscatholic.org). *U.S. Catholic* is published by the Claretians. For subscriptions, call 1–800–328–6515 or visit uscatholic.org.

Earlier versions of Chapters 10, 11, and 12 were published by St. Anthony Messenger Press, © Copyright 2011 and 2009, respectively, 28 W. Liberty Street, Cincinnati, OH 45202. 800–488–0488. www.AmericanCatholic.org. All rights reserved.

Part of the content of Chapters 12 and 13 is from *Keeping the Seasons: Reproducibles for Lent-Triduum-Easter 2010,* © 2009, Archdiocese of Chicago, Liturgy Training Publications, www.LTP.org. Used with permission. All rights reserved.

Part of Chapter 13 appeared originally in *Liguorian,* April 2000, 11–12.

Chapter 16 was first published as "God's Glorious Nobodies," in St. Anthony Messenger Press, November 1, 2011. Slightly edited for the current publication.

Chapter 17 was originally published as "A People Ahead of Their Time" in the *National Catholic Reporter,* May 26, 2011.

Chapter 18 was originally published as "Spanish Lessons" in *U.S. Catholic* 74, no. 6 (June 2009) and is reprinted by permission.

Chapter 19 first appeared as "Amazon Warrior: Dorothy Stang" in *U.S. Catholic* 73, no. 4 (April 1, 2008) and is reprinted by permission.

Chapter 20 was originally published as "Duo's Music Brings Contagious Cheer" in the *National Catholic Reporter* (NCRonline.org), September 9, 2010.

Chapter 21 first appeared as "U.S. Sisters Have Served with Grace and Fidelity" in the *National Catholic Reporter* (NCRonline.org), September 11, 2009.

Chapter 24 was originally published as "Spirituality: What's Your Style?" in the *Catholic Update* (AmericanCatholic.org), March 2009.